The Ploughman's Lunch and the Miser's Feast

The PLOUGHMAN'S LUNCH
and the MISER'S FEAST

*Authentic Pub Food, Restaurant Fare, and Home Cooking
from Small Towns, Big Cities, and Country Villages Across the British Isles*

BRIAN YARVIN

THE HARVARD COMMON PRESS
BOSTON, MASSACHUSETTS

The Harvard Common Press
535 Albany Street
Boston, Massachusetts 02118
www.harvardcommonpress.com

Printed in China
Printed on acid-free paper

Library of Congress Cataloging-in-Publication Data
Yarvin, Brian.
The ploughman's lunch and the miser's feast : authentic pub food, restaurant fare, and home cooking from small towns, big cities, and country villages across the British Isles / Brian Yarvin.
p. cm.
Includes index.
ISBN 978-1-55832-413-8 (hardback : acid-free paper)
1. Cooking, English. 2. Cooking--Scotland. 3. Cookbooks. I. Title.
TX717.Y37 2012
641.5942--dc23
2011025958

Portions of the sidebar "Pie, Mash, Liquor, and Maybe Some Eels, Too" first appeared in *The Washington Post* on February 14, 2010.
Portions of the sidebar "Deep-Fried Candy Bars" first appeared on SeriousEats.com on June 8, 2009.

Special bulk-order discounts are available on this and other Harvard Common Press books.
Companies and organizations may purchase books for premiums or resale,
or may arrange a custom edition, by contacting the Marketing Director at the address above.

Jacket photographs, front: Banoffee Pie, page 169; *back:* Cawl (Welsh Lamb Stew), page 71, and Chicken and Leek Casserole, page 76

Jacket photography and prop styling by Sabra Krock; food styling by Mariana Velasquez
Book design by Elizabeth Van Itallie

10 9 8 7 6 5 4 3 2 1

For the farmers, food vendors, and cooks of Great Britain—
the unsung heroes of an unsung cuisine

Contents

Discovering British Food: An Introduction.. viii

A Full Breakfast.. 2

Sandwiches, Salads, and Small Plates.. 14

The Soup Pot.. 40

The Main Course.. 58

The Curry Shop.. 100

On the Side.. 120

Savory Pies and Baked Goods.. 134

The Sweet Side.. 162

The Ploughman's Cupboard.. 188

A Modest Glossary of British Food Terms.. 198

Acknowledgments.. 202

Measurement Equivalents.. 203

Index.. 204

THE 12 DAYS OF CHRISTMAS
FOOD MARKET
COVENT GARDEN LONDON

BOOKS

*Left: Tenby, Wales;
upper right: Covent
Garden, London; bottom
right: Notting Hill
Market, London*

Discovering British Food:
An Introduction

For all too long, we Americans were supposed to think that British food was awful. How did we know? It was easy! The British themselves told us whenever they had the chance. Those of us who had been to Great Britain didn't always disagree. Dinners in the mess halls of rural hostels, hurried lunches at dingy train stations, and breakfasts that featured three sad-looking versions of fried swine were hard to argue with.

Even twenty years ago, change was in the air. The pungent spices of South Asia had penetrated even to small towns in the UK, and everybody and their neighbors had eaten fine food in France or Italy, sipped coffee in Seattle, and perhaps even tasted some of those Asian flavors in their countries of origin. The British palate was growing up.

Word of this transformation reached our shores suddenly and without warning. One day, we flipped on our televisions and "Two Fat Ladies" were telling us how wonderful British food was. Before we could fully recover, there was Jamie Oliver with his cool friends, his giant chopping block, and the exact same message: Great Britain was the place for food.

Nowadays we look upon a raging Gordon Ramsay with awe and return from Britain longing for British beef, or a great curry, and a glass of pulled ale to wash it all down.

How the world changes! And, yet, some things don't. To this day, none of my British friends will admit that their vast food revolution actually happened. Only grudgingly will they concede that Jamie is a global celebrity at least in part for his cooking skills, or that all that attention to artisanal, organic, and local ingredients has resulted in at least a few items that taste really good.

So, when my British friends heard that I wanted to write about the traditional foods of their country, instead of writing yet another cookbook about pasta, pizza, risotto, or grilling, they were a bit shocked—and maybe a bit embarrassed. Did I really have to remind the rest of the English-speaking world that in the UK they still eat baked beans for breakfast? Indeed, that they still *enjoy* eating baked beans for breakfast? Yes, they blushed a bit when I mentioned the great seafood, meats, and produce, or the joy of a Sunday afternoon roast beef platter in a rural pub. They admitted the existence of interesting local specialties like pasties and

oatcakes. But only now are they coming around to the idea that all these foods and dishes together make up a fresh, new, and vibrant food culture.

Even though the best artisanal products in Britain easily equal the best from its neighbors, we're not yet at the point where we say, to someone who has returned from Great Britain, "Wow! You went to Devon. Did you bring back some cream?" That day is coming, though. In the meantime, bake a steak and kidney pie or some pasties, follow them with a fruit trifle, and wash it all down with some real ale. You won't be sorry.

A
FULL
BREAKFAST

"**D**o you require breakfast?" is a question you will often hear when booking a room in Great Britain. The question may be worded a bit strangely to American ears, but it's about the meal that counts above all others. *Bedand-breakfast* never means a bed and a bowl of corn flakes. It means a bed and a meal so extensive that it's almost a state of mind.

the full english: a breakfast for the ages

Every hotel, bed-and-breakfast, tea shop, café, and all-day pub claims to serve something called the full English breakfast. Just what is it? After eating a few hundred of them, I feel that I can offer some insight. The meal always includes at least one egg, toast, and a minimum of one fried breakfast meat, such as bacon or sausage. But there's more. A breakfast plate will almost always have baked beans and other extras, such as cooked mushrooms, fried or grilled tomatoes, and slices of fried bread. There will frequently be fruit and cold cereal, too.

A full breakfast is a declaration of Britishness, in the same way a meal with pasta first and meat afterwards means you're in Italy. Get breakfast in a place like Gibraltar, and you'll know who's in charge; when a flight attendant serves you one, there's no question about the plane's home base. And the decline of British train travel can be traced to the moment that the full breakfast ceased being served on board.

Here's a breakdown of what you'll need for a full breakfast. The more of these items you have, the more British you'll be. There are no distinct courses; you just get it all out there at the same time and show everybody that the day is ready to start.

Eggs. If you say nothing in a British eatery, they'll come to you fried over easy. But they can be prepared in any way. Poached and soft-boiled are not unusual requests.

Sausage. Typically a milder version of American breakfast sausage, it can be fried or grilled. It ranges from cocktail- to hot dog–size.

Bacon. British bacon is from a leaner cut of the pig and has much less fat than American bacon. Like American bacon it is cured, but it is not always smoked. You can sometimes find it in American groceries, where it's sold as "British" or "Irish" bacon.

Baked beans. Similar to American canned "vegetarian beans," they seem to play the same role that hash browns do in the States. I offer my recipe on page 7.

Mushrooms. Typically button mushrooms, either fried in butter or poached in a bit of water, and never seasoned heavily.

Tomatoes. Plum tomatoes, always described on menus as "grilled," even though they're often broiled.

Toast. Absolutely essential. The ideal bread is baked in a loaf pan, dense, and close grained.

Fried bread. Slices of white bread that are pan-fried, usually in bacon fat or margarine. In the bigger kitchens of cafés and restaurants, it might be deep-fried.

Kippers. Split, gutted, salted, and smoked herring, which would seem familiar to anybody who ate in Jewish delis in New York City forty years ago. In England they're often served filleted and fried in butter.

Black pudding. What Americans call blood sausage. In the UK, it's made from pig's blood, with cereal as a filler. Black pudding is more common in the north, but it can show up on a breakfast menu almost anywhere in the British Isles.

Kedgeree. Perhaps named for and rooted in the Indian dish *kitchri*, it's a mixture of rice, flaked fish, and boiled eggs. It's often made today with curry powder.

Beverages are also an important part of the experience and are often your first clue to the quality of the meal. Coffee in a plunger pot is always a good sign. American diner–style brewers with glass carafes mean that at least you won't get instant. (Often the British will request instant coffee even when excellent fresh-brewed java is put in front of them.) Tea at breakfast time falls within a narrow range. It's never all that bad, but I have yet to be served an excellent pot in a full English breakfast.

FRIED BREAD

Makes 4 servings

People in the UK love their fried food so much that they even prepare plain old bread this way. Needless to say, this dish wasn't invented by some grease fanatic. The custom began with poor families, who put some bread in a hot pan that had just been used to cook bacon. Even after the liquid was poured off, there was still some fat and flavor clinging to the pan, and what would be better than bread to absorb it? Since British bacon is much leaner these days, the pan is almost dry when you finish cooking it; hence the need for the added fat in this recipe. But the spirit of thrift, and the desire to make every meal as filling as possible, remain.

3 tablespoons butter or margarine
8 slices sandwich bread

1. Melt enough of the butter in a heavy skillet (preferably the same one in which you have just fried some British bacon) over medium heat to coat the bottom of the pan.

2. Lay a few slices of bread in the pan, and cook them, flipping them occasionally, until both sides are golden, about 6 minutes total. Repeat with additional butter and the remaining slices of bread. Serve right away with eggs, bacon, and plenty of hot tea.

British-Style Baked Beans

Makes 8 servings

I am served baked beans at breakfast almost every day I am in England. Each time I put a forkful in my mouth, I think, "I could do a lot better than this." Of course, when I try to discuss it with people, they are mystified—no one thinks of baked beans as being a cooked dish or having component ingredients. They are just something that comes out of a can.

2 cups dried navy beans
1 tablespoon vegetable oil
1 tablespoon mustard powder
2 teaspoons salt
1 teaspoon freshly ground black pepper
1 cup diced onion
½ cup chopped red bell pepper
1 cup chopped celery
1 (28-ounce) can crushed tomatoes
5 cloves
2 tablespoons cider vinegar
¼ cup unsulphured molasses
⅓ cup packed dark brown sugar
2 cups water

1. Preheat the oven to 350°F. Put the beans in a deep bowl, cover with at least 3 inches of water, and soak for at least 8 hours, or overnight. Rinse and drain the beans.

2. Combine the oil, mustard, salt, and pepper in a Dutch oven or a large ovenproof pot over medium heat and cook, stirring, for 15 seconds or until the mustard is absorbed by the oil. Add the onion, bell pepper, and celery and continue cooking until the onion becomes translucent, about 10 minutes.

3. Add the soaked beans, tomatoes, cloves, vinegar, molasses, brown sugar, and water and stir until the mixture is well combined and the sugar has dissolved. Cover the pot and transfer it to your oven.

4. Bake the beans for 6 hours, stirring every 30 minutes or so. If the beans start drying out, add a bit of water. The dish is ready when the beans have a creamy texture.

bed-and-breakfasts

Wherever you go in the world these days, you'll see "B & B" or "Bed-and-Breakfast" establishments. They may be everywhere now, but they originated—and still exist in their purest form—in the UK. In their most perfect state, they're regular private homes with a few rooms to rent for overnight guests. The owner offers you tea when you get in, and, the next morning, cooks you a huge breakfast, the sort of breakfast that the British dream of eating on their own vacations, and sends you on your way.

The worst can be off-putting, with strange smells, perhaps, or bizarrely ornate furniture. For many, an in-room bathroom (called "en-suite" in B & B jargon) is the most important feature. This has forced many otherwise nice rooms to have strange compact toilets and showers crammed in. I'd much rather have a full bath with a large tub across the hall, but maybe that's just me.

The best British bed-and-breakfast inns are clean but not so fussy that you feel like a slob the moment you walk in the door. They offer a good tea tray and a friendly tone in the morning. You'll walk out of these places feeling well-fed and well-rested. Not a bad way to start the day.

Tenby, Wales

KEDGEREE

Makes 4 servings

A traditional pilaf made with smoked fish, rice, Indian spices, and a garnish of hard-cooked eggs, kedgeree might not seem like something you would want first thing in the morning. But the British enjoy it, and once you've gotten used to those big breakfasts, you'll feel the same way. Like almost everything on a full English breakfast menu, kedgeree also makes a great lunch or dinner dish. Note that although curry paste is almost always made in the UK, American supermarkets put it in the Indian section. Your local Indian grocer will carry it for half the price in any case.

1 cup whole milk
4 ounces smoked haddock or kipper fillets, chopped
1 tablespoon unsalted butter
½ cup chopped onion
1 tablespoon mild curry paste
1 cup basmati rice
3 cups low-sodium chicken broth
2 tablespoons chopped fresh flat-leaf parsley
2 hard-cooked eggs, halved lengthwise

1. Pour the milk into a large saucepan and bring it to a simmer over low heat. Add the fish and let it cook for 5 minutes, or until it has given up some of its salt and you can see some brown bits separating out into the milk. Drain the fish and set it aside.

2. Melt the butter in a large skillet over medium heat and sauté the onion until it turns translucent, about 10 minutes. Add the curry paste and mix well.

3. Add the rice to the skillet and stir until the grains are well coated with onion mixture. Pour in the chicken broth, turn up the heat to high, and boil for 1 minute.

4. Add the fish, stir to mix the ingredients well, and reduce the heat so the broth is simmering. Cover and cook, undisturbed, for 20 minutes, or until all the liquid is absorbed by the rice.

5. Add the parsley. Stir the kedgeree one more time so that all the ingredients are well combined, garnish with the eggs, and serve.

BLACK PUDDING

Makes 1 or 2 large puddings, to serve 4

If you can't stand the sight of blood, stop right here. Black pudding is indeed made from congealed blood. But this is nothing more than the British version of a dish that was once eaten everywhere in the world, and is still prized in many places.

Of course, in order to make this, you're going to need some pig, lamb, or cow blood, which may be easier to find than you think. Big Chinese supermarkets always seem to have pints of frozen pig blood, which is perfect for whipping up a batch of black pudding. With a bit of pestering, you might be able to talk your local butcher (or even a local slaughterhouse, if there is one) into saving some for you, too. For filling sausage casings, a sausage stuffer is best, but a serving spoon is fine. Note that the sausages will need at least 8 hours in the refrigerator to firm up.

2 large natural sausage casings ("hog middles" in
  butcher's jargon)
4 cups pig, lamb, or cow blood
1 cup shredded beef suet
1 cup whole milk
1 cup rolled oats (not instant)
2 cups finely chopped onion
2 teaspoons salt
1 teaspoon freshly ground black pepper
1 teaspoon dried sage
1 teaspoon cayenne pepper
1 teaspoon dried thyme
½ teaspoon ground nutmeg
3 tablespoons butter, oil, or bacon fat, for frying

1. Soak the sausage casings in a bowl of warm water for a few moments, and then give them a good rinse, inside and out. Drain and set aside.

2. Stir together the blood, suet, milk, oats, onion, salt, pepper, sage, cayenne, thyme, and nutmeg in a large bowl. Make sure all the solid ingredients are evenly distributed.

3. Tie off one end of a sausage casing and use a sausage stuffer or spoon to fill with the blood mixture. Do not pack it too tightly, or it will burst when you cook it. Tie the open end closed with butcher's twine.

4. Place the filled sausages in a steamer basket. Place the basket in a pot with a couple of inches of simmering water, and steam the sausages, covered, until they are cooked all the way through, about 1½ hours.

5. Remove the sausages from the heat and put in the refrigerator for at least 8 hours to solidify properly.

6. Before serving, heat the frying fat in a large skillet over medium-high heat. Slice the sausages ½ inch thick, and fry on both sides until they begin to brown, about 4 minutes total. Serve warm as part of a big breakfast. The blood pudding will keep in the refrigerator for up to 1 week.

JUGGED KIPPERS
Makes 4 servings

First of all, what is a kipper? It's a salted and smoked herring, which is traditionally eaten in northern England, on the Isle of Man, and in Scotland. You can find similar salted and smoked herrings all over northern Europe.

Next, what is jugging? It is a method of cooking food by soaking it in boiling-hot water, off the heat source. Jugged kippers are that simple. Make sure you have whole salted fish, and not canned fillets. They aren't the easiest items to find, but there are more than a few Internet sources. Specialty smoked-fish shops and gourmet shops occasionally have them, too.

4 whole kippers
1 lemon, quartered
Toast, for serving

1. Use a good, sharp pair of kitchen scissors to cut the head, tail, and fins away from the fish. Lay the fish in a heatproof bowl or baking dish.

2. Pour enough boiling water over the fish just to cover them. Let them soak for 5 minutes. Drain them, pat them dry, and place on small plates. Serve the kippers immediately with the lemon wedges and toast at breakfast or anytime you like.

Scotch Woodcock

Makes 2 servings

If you are expecting to find instructions on how to roast a game bird, you'll have to search elsewhere. The dish known as Scotch woodcock is a sort of seasoned scrambled eggs. How did it get this very misleading name? Unfortunately, I have no idea.

4 large eggs
½ cup whole milk
2 tablespoons capers, rinsed and drained
2 tablespoons chopped fresh flat-leaf parsley
1 tablespoon unsalted butter
4 slices sandwich bread, toasted
2 tablespoons anchovy paste
4 anchovy fillets
Hot sauce, for serving

1. Combine the eggs, milk, capers, and parsley in a large bowl and whisk until all the ingredients are well blended.

2. Melt the butter in a nonstick skillet over medium-low heat. Pour in the egg mixture and cook, stirring occasionally, until the eggs are just about set, about 10 minutes.

3. Spread the toast with the anchovy paste and put 2 on each of two plates. Spoon the cooked egg mixture on the toast and place an anchovy fillet on each mound of eggs. Serve warm, with a dash of hot sauce.

GRILLED TOMATOES

Makes 4 servings

Grilled tomatoes have always been part of a full English breakfast (see page 4), but I had never been able to find the grill in the restaurant kitchen or the grill marks on the tomatoes. I eventually learned that *grilled* really meant roasted. So here is a recipe for British-style "grilled" tomatoes.

4 medium-size tomatoes, halved crosswise
1 teaspoon salt
½ teaspoon freshly ground black pepper

1. Preheat the oven to 425°F. Spray a cookie sheet with cooking spray and place the tomatoes cut side up on it. Sprinkle with the salt and pepper.

2. Roast the tomatoes for 40 minutes, or until they have started to brown at the edges and have lost some of their shape. Let them cool for a few minutes and serve warm.

a big breakfast anywhere

I had always been vaguely aware that it was possible to fly to London from the States in the morning, but I had never done it. In over twenty years of regular transatlantic travel, I took it for granted that a person took off in the evening and landed at their UK destination at the crack of dawn.

Then one day my wife, Maria, announced a big surprise: Our upcoming Newark-to-London flight would be departing at eight in the morning. My first thought was, Doesn't this mean we have to wake up at four? After realizing that this was indeed true, and that Maria didn't care, I packed my bags, set the alarm clock, and was up as promised.

At the gate there wasn't much to eat, and I was pretty upset. Of course I needn't have worried. Soon after takeoff, a flight attendant on the Britain-based carrier asked me if I wanted a "full English" or "just an omelet." I jumped at the "full," and as it was being placed in front of me, I realized I was no longer the least bit upset about having to get up at four.

On my tray was an Englishman's dream. One plate held scrambled eggs, hash browns, a sausage, a rasher of real British bacon (how did they find that at Newark Airport?), and a roasted tomato. On another plate sat a couple of slices of cold ham and Swiss cheese. Also on that tray were a hard roll, butter, a muffin, granola, strawberry yogurt, orange juice, a fruit cup, a bottle of water, and a small Cadbury chocolate bar. Soon the flight attendant returned with tea so strong I mistook it for coffee. By the time we were halfway through our eggs, we discovered that our "in-flight entertainment systems" offered several of my wife's favorite home-remodeling and real-estate TV shows. We could easily have been in a small-town B & B breakfast room in Britain. We were treated to a bit of the Queen's England before we had even passed over Cape Cod.

SANDWICHES, SALADS, and SMALL PLATES

T he British are masters of the sandwich. They invented them and have now spent several hundred years perfecting them. British snacks are less well known, but well worth trying.

There are eggs, as a matter of course. Try them cold as pickled eggs or deep-fried as Scotch eggs; you'll find recipes for both in this chapter. How about jellied fish cream, kipper pâté, or deviled crab? And a sandwich of salmon and cucumber or coronation chicken is always welcome. Staffordshire oatcakes, which we would now call a street food, are unsung heroes of the local foods movement. Don't forget that pot of tea, though. It goes with everything.

MENU

Thai Chicken Noodle Soup — 2.50
LENTIL & VEG SOUP 2.50
Homemade Lasagne or Veg Lasagne 5.75
Steak Pie with Veg & Chips 5.75
Salmon & Asparagus Quiche with Baked Potato 5
Vegetable Quiche or Chips
Chicken Tikka Rice & Poppadoms 5.75
Fish Chips & Peas 5.75
Stovies & Oatcakes 4.75
BURGERS
Beef, Chicken, Haggis, Veggie

HOMEBAKING   Bacon Roll 1.75
Scones   Egg Roll 1.75
Cakes   Sausage Roll 1.75
Pancakes   Beans on Toast 2.75
Gateaux   Poached Egg on Toast 2.95
Meringues   Scrambled Egg on Toast 2.95
Sponges   ALL DAY BREAKFAST 3.75

ALL HOMEMADE

HOT & COLD
MEALS
SERVED
DAILY

All Day Breakfast
Steak Pie
Beef Lasagne
Stovies and Oatcakes
Scampi and chips
Macaroni Cheese

~ Homemade ~
Scones, Cakes & Bakes

tea: the drink

While here in the States, I found myself in need of some serious counsel. Although my wife brewed tea from leaves even when she just wanted a quick cup, every attempt I'd made ended in disaster. Sometimes I got an inky liquid that was wonderfully suited to calligraphy, and at other times I ended up with a thin broth that tasted like, well, leaves. I decided I needed to consult an expert. Judith Krall-Russo, an American author and tea educator, was just such a person. I sat down with Judith—over tea, of course—to learn more about the subject.

I began with the most basic question: How do you turn those little black leaves into a real cup of tea? She told me that she always begins with fresh cold or room-temperature water—never previously heated or boiled—and brings it just to the boiling point. First, she said, splash a bit in the pot and spill it out; this warms the pot. Then add 1 teaspoon of tea leaves for each cup to the pot, and pour in about one-quarter of the water you'll be making the tea with. Let this concentrate steep for about 5 minutes. Finally, Judith instructed, dilute the steeped tea with the remaining water, and serve it right away.

When I asked Judith about stainless-steel tea balls, which I've always thought of as one of the best cheap gifts, she was horrified. It turns out that the stainless isn't a good material and the small size of the tea balls prevents the tea leaves from expanding properly. I was crushed. No, I never use tea balls myself, but I really meant well when I gave them to people!

Next I asked Judith to tell me what the difference is between a tea and a high tea. For that matter I wondered, Is there such a thing as a low tea? Judith brightened as if she'd been waiting all her life for somebody to ask her these questions. "A high tea is one served at a dining room table that is high enough to require you to sit upright," she said. "And a low tea is one served on what we Americans would call a coffee table, a low table in front of a sofa or easy chair." Obvious, right?

Soon the conversation drifted to the American perception of an English tea—a formal meal of sandwiches and sweets, often held in faux Victorian surroundings—when the reality is that the British drink their tea anywhere at any time and with any sort of food. Yes, the British will sometimes call their evening meal tea (see Pie for Tea on page 136) and, yes, you can have tea in pretty fancy surroundings. It's just that it's not typical. And no, it doesn't have to be at four o'clock, a common misconception.

Judith is a tea idealist. She reminded me that a properly brewed pot of tea is a form of meditation, a comfort, and a way of "coming into the moment," as she put it. When you travel in Britain, tea is like a special form of refreshment. You might dream of a beer or two while on a long walk, but Judith is right: What really refreshes you at the end of the trail is a pot of tea.

When I was at Judith's that afternoon, along with the tea she served lovely little bread and jam sandwiches, which were trimmed with a cookie cutter into the shape of a teapot. They were lots of fun, but you don't need to make such an effort when you serve tea. Bread, butter, and jam are the perfect accompaniment, whatever shape they're in. As Judith drank tea with me, she became more thoughtful about the drink itself. She pointed to her tea and said, "People look at that cup, and they want a good cup of tea. They expect a cup of tea when they're happy, and when they're sad, they need a cup of tea to discuss it over."

Driving home that day, I realized that the spirit of tea resides equally in a graceful pot of tea brewed by a master like Judith and in a modest tea bag dropped into water that's been boiled on a hot plate. It's the drink that mountain climbers sipped after planting the Union Jack on the summit of a far-off peak, and the one a London cabdriver has when he's on break. It can be served elegantly in a Cotswold village shop, or offered in a plastic cup on a train. More than any other, it's the drink that defines Britain. After all, can you imagine a cricketer sipping an espresso?

CORONATION CHICKEN

Makes 4 salad servings or 6 sandwiches

The coronation of Queen Elizabeth II in 1953 was, as you well might imagine, a big event. But you may not be familiar with the coronation's culinary legacy. The chicken salad seasoned with curry that was served that day has become one of England's signature dishes.

1 tablespoon peanut oil
½ cup chopped onion
1 teaspoon mild curry paste
1 teaspoon tomato paste
2 tablespoons red wine
2 tablespoons fresh lemon juice
1 bay leaf
1 cup drained and finely chopped canned apricot
1 cup mayonnaise
2 tablespoons heavy cream
3 cups chopped cooked chicken (about 1¼ pounds)
1 teaspoon salt
½ teaspoon freshly ground white pepper
2 tablespoons chopped watercress

1. Combine the oil and onion in a skillet over medium heat and cook the onion, stirring occasionally, until it is tender, about 10 minutes.

2. Mix in the curry paste, tomato paste, wine, lemon juice, and bay leaf. Reduce the heat to medium-low and cook, stirring frequently, until the liquid evaporates and the onion mixture is a thick paste, about 15 minutes. Remove from the heat and remove the bay leaf.

3. Combine the onion mixture with the apricot, mayonnaise, cream, chicken, salt, and pepper in a large bowl and mix well. Cover and let it sit in the refrigerator for at least 2 hours so the flavors can meld. Finally, garnish with the watercress. Serve chilled either on salad plates or in sandwiches.

JELLIED FISH CREAM

Makes 4 servings

These molded gelatin dishes may remind you of the 1950s, but in the UK they're part of a long tradition. This recipe, which really does contain gelatin, fish, and cream, dates back at least one hundred years. The British think of it as a classic, rather than a relic.

1 (14½-ounce) can salmon
1 cup dry white wine
2 cups fish stock or low-sodium chicken broth
2 packets plain gelatin powder (about ¼ cup)
½ cup heavy cream
1 cup frozen green peas, thawed
¼ cup chopped fresh flat-leaf parsley
1 teaspoon salt
½ teaspoon freshly ground black pepper

1. Drain the salmon and use a fork to flake and mash it. Set it aside.

2. Pour the wine and stock into a saucepan over medium-high heat and bring just to a simmer. Remove from the heat and let the mixture cool to lukewarm.

3. Sprinkle the gelatin powder on the surface of the wine-stock mixture and let stand undisturbed for 10 minutes. Then stir until all the powder has dissolved.

4. This calls for some careful observation: Pour the gelatin liquid into a large bowl and chill in the refrigerator until it just begins to solidify. This takes about 1 hour in my refrigerator, but I suggest you check it every 15 minutes in yours to make sure. It should be thick enough to hold the solid ingredients, but not so thick that they just sit on top.

5. Stir the salmon, cream, peas, parsley, salt, and pepper into the gelatin mixture. If you add these ingredients before the gelatin begins to solidify, they will settle at the bottom; and if you wait until it's too solid, stirring in these ingredients will yield a chopped-up mess.

6. Pour the mixture into a 5- or 6-cup mold and chill for at least 2 hours. Unmold onto a serving dish, slice, and serve cold.

GALANTINE *of* CHICKEN

Makes 6 servings

Need a chicken dish for a picnic, potluck, or buffet? A galantine, which resembles a large, round meatloaf, will do the job perfectly. Serve it warm right away or make it a day or two ahead and serve cold.

1 cup chopped British or Canadian bacon (see sidebar, page 91)
1 pound boneless, skinless chicken breast, cut into 1-inch pieces
8 ounces mild bulk sausage
1 cup dried, unflavored bread crumbs
½ teaspoon dried sage
½ teaspoon ground mace
3 tablespoons chopped fresh flat-leaf parsley
1 large egg
1 teaspoon salt
½ teaspoon freshly ground black pepper

1. Combine the bacon and chicken in a food processor and pulse until the meats become a coarse paste.

2. Combine the bacon-chicken mixture with the sausage, bread crumbs, sage, mace, 2 tablespoons of the parsley, egg, salt, and pepper in a large bowl. Stir well to make sure the ingredients are evenly distributed.

3. Oil a 6-cup heatproof round bowl and pack with the meat mixture. Because the galantine will be unmolded in the bowl shape, try to keep the top (which will become the bottom) of the mixture level; use a butter knife or spatula if needed. Cover with aluminum foil.

4. To steam, pour about 1 inch of water into a large pot with a cover. Then put the foil-covered bowl in the pot. The bowl should be near, but not touching, the water. (I use a 5-inch ring mold.) Finally, cover the pot itself and place over low heat so the water simmers. The galantine will need about 2 hours to cook all the way through. It's done when a long toothpick or bamboo skewer inserted in the center comes out dry.

5. Remove the galantine from the pot and let it cool in the bowl until it is easy to handle, about 15 minutes. Unmold it onto a serving plate by flipping it over and tapping gently on the bottom of the bowl. Garnish with the remaining tablespoon of parsley. If you're serving the galantine warm, serve it immediately. If serving cold, chill, tightly covered, in the refrigerator for at least 2 hours or up to several days.

pilgrimage: **smoking permitted**

Stonington, Maine, is a pretty remote place. To get there, you'll have to leave the main highway, drive for miles down hilly side roads, and then cross a surprisingly large suspension bridge and a causeway. When you get there, though, there's more than a bit of Maine at its best: a perfect harbor with fishing boats, small shops selling what fishermen need, and trucks ready to get that fish to market. This is where Richard Penfold has set up shop. Yes, there are a few art galleries and espresso bars, too, but they don't ruin the experience. All in all, it's the perfect place to run a fish-smoking business.

You wouldn't expect a guru of kippers and finnan haddie to be in the United States, but from his outpost in Stonington, Richard produces some of the world's finest smoked fish. Originally from London and schooled in Plymouth, Richard spent more than a decade in places like the Shetland Islands learning the art of smoking fish and becoming an expert on every aspect of commercial fishing. While in the Shetlands, he taught at the North Atlantic Fisheries College and created their fish-processing library. This is a man whose life is truly focused.

When I visited Richard on a cold winter's day, we were soon talking about the proper way to defrost frozen fish. A few moments later, Richard confirmed something I'd long suspected—that quality frozen fish is far better than a lot of fresh fish that's available, and that frozen fish finds its way into many of the finest kitchens.

He'd prepped three or four kinds of fish and was mixing up a brine of salt and water. "Brine is immensely powerful stuff," he said while moving fillets through the bath. I was used to brining pork and turkey and thought a few days was about right. Richard brined the fish fillets for *80 seconds*. According to Richard, understanding brining is the key to the process. It was the length of time in the brine that determined how salty the final product would be.

Richard was trying to teach me about the entire North Atlantic fishery and the science of fish handling in a single day, and I was just trying to wrap my mind around notions like "finnan haddie is made out of

haddock" and "kippers are made from the same herring they sell in Polish grocery stores." As we went through the day, I came to realize that this was a country boy moving at city boy speed. One minute he'd be filleting fish and washing down the counter, and the next he'd be at the kiln getting the smoke going, or using specially cleaned needle-nose pliers to pull pin bones from salmon.

Hidden in the dead center of the operation is that kiln, a bathroom-size, highly controllable smoking unit. I asked Richard what sort of wood he used. "We get food-grade sawdust from Virginia," he told me. I imagined that the sawdust from those Maine loggers would do a good job, and, as usual, I was wrong. "You can't have wood that was just cut by some guy's chainsaw," he explained. "It's been splattered with oil. You don't know what's in it."

"Good grief," I thought. Details! Details!

Soon the steps became clear: First the fish is prepped. The haddock for the finnan haddie is filleted, and the kippers are split in half, with their bones left in. Then the fish is brined—that is, immersed in the salt solution for that quick 80-second dip. And after that it's smoked in a kiln for a couple of hours, cooled, and packaged for sale.

By midafternoon, the kilns were filled with smoking fish and the pace was winding down. Richard was hinting that I should leave the building for an hour or so. It was obvious that some secret ritual was going on, and I was determined to find out what it was. I later learned that Richard is a huge Terry Gross fan and it was time for her National Public Radio show.

That night I joined Richard and a few others for dinner at his home. We had fish, of course. In fact, it was some of the same Icelandic haddock he'd shown me that morning. The conversation was mostly about fish, and Richard, a self-described "fish-head," liked it that way.

What was it like moving from the Shetlands to Stonington, I asked. "The Shetlands were far more remote," Richard said, "and you could be cut off for days from the mainland. Here, we're connected by a suspension bridge. And the weather, it's colder in the winter in Maine, but the Shetlands feel more severe. Especially on days when the boats can't come over." His American wife may have had to push him a bit when they first decided to come, but they seemed pretty content on that bitter cold night.

After I left, I noticed that both my clothes and my car gave off a sublime fragrance: smoke from Richard's kilns. Nothing fishy, and as pristine as Maine itself.

KIPPER PÂTÉ

Makes 1 cup, to serve 4

Kippers, those intensely flavored smoked and salted fish, may be hard to eat straight up—even the British don't seem to do so. But they are great with just a bit of extra preparation, and this pâté is a perfect example. While it's not exactly like a French pâté, you can smear it on a bagel, warm toast, or a good dark bread.

8 ounces kipper fillets
4 tablespoons (½ stick) unsalted butter, at room
  temperature
2 tablespoons heavy cream
1 tablespoon fresh lemon juice
¼ teaspoon salt
¼ teaspoon freshly ground black pepper
¼ teaspoon chili powder
½ teaspoon Worcestershire sauce
2 tablespoons chopped scallion (green part only)
2 tablespoons chopped fresh flat-leaf parsley

1. Combine the kippers, butter, cream, lemon juice, salt, pepper, chili powder, and Worcestershire sauce in the bowl of a food processor and process the mixture into a thick paste.

2. Add the scallion and parsley, and pulse a few times so that the greens are evenly distributed but not pureed.

3. Transfer to a large dish with a lid, such as a terrine. The pâté should be served at room temperature. Serve it right away, or store in the refrigerator, covered with the lid, for later. Several hours before you're ready to serve, take the pâté out of the refrigerator so it will soften.

the ploughman's lunch

The ploughman's lunch is one of those dishes whose origins are not quite what they seem. These light and elegant plates are unlikely to be the fare of hard-working ploughmen or, for that matter, of any farmers at all. Indeed, one legend has it that the name and concept originated with a 1930s advertising campaign. Whatever its history may be, you can order it in almost any British pub with a kitchen. Here's what you'll get: a large piece of cheese or cold meat, some salad, some bread with butter, and a serving of chutney, one of England's many Indian-inspired condiments.

Those of you familiar with the ubiquitous Greek salad of American diner fame will understand the role of the ploughman's lunch perfectly. It's lighter than anything roasted or fried, yet the chunk of protein gives the meal substance. It's a platter that imparts a vague impression of healthy eating— as long as you don't start thinking about the sugar in the chutney, the fat in the cheese, and all that butter that comes with the bread.

Assembling a ploughman is easy. Each portion should have 4 to 6 ounces of one cheese or meat, 2 or 3 cups of mixed greens, a slice of tomato, some pickled onions or gherkins, a bit of chutney, and a side of rolls and butter.

Some thoughts on the ingredients:

Cheese. The perfect candidate is a wedge of an artisanal farmhouse cheddar. Try for something English, and serve it at room temperature. No cheese is so good that it's palatable in a congealed, frigid block.

Cold meat. Pubs often serve a single thick slice of cooked ham or rare roast beef. At its best, the ham is neither soggy nor gelatinous. Look for a consistent pink color and a bit of fat around the edges. The roast beef could easily be left over, or it may be cooked for the occasion. Either way, it should be rosy in

the center and deep brown at the edges. You can leave a bit of fat around it. According to the logic of a ploughman's lunch, it's canceled out by the salad next to it.

Salad. Fresh mixed baby greens will do the trick well. Add a bit of arugula to give it a base of strong flavor. Wedges of tomato, slices of cucumber, a bit of shredded carrot, perhaps a few small gherkins, and a garnish of fruit can all be added. Dressing is usually on the side.

Chutney. See the recipe on page 195. If you are buying a prepared version, look for Major Grey's. This is a flavor variety, not a brand.

Bread. Try to find some really crusty rolls. Mini baguettes are popular, but round or oval roll shapes are seen, too. Make sure there's nothing soft or cottony about the bread. In Britain, bread always comes with butter.

Arrange the items in separate piles on a large plate and serve. Needless to say, a ploughman cries for a pint of beer or hard cider (in Britain, *cider* always means hard cider) alongside.

PICKLED EGGS

Makes 1 dozen eggs

Some modern British pubs offer menus that rival French restaurants, but old-time places will not have more than a few packets of crunchy snacks and a big jar of pickled eggs. These pickled eggs are refrigerator pickles; there's no canning involved.

- 1 dozen large eggs
- 4 cups cider vinegar
- 1 tablespoon black peppercorns
- 5 whole cloves

1. Hard-cook the eggs by immersing them in simmering water for 10 minutes. Set aside and let cool.

2. Combine the vinegar, peppercorns, and cloves in a saucepan and boil for 1 minute. Set aside and let cool.

3. Peel the eggs and put them in a nonreactive container with a tight-fitting lid. Add the vinegar-spice mixture and stir very gently to make sure the liquid moistens every part of every egg. Cover and refrigerate. The eggs will be pickled and ready to eat after 3 days. They will keep, refrigerated, for up to 2 more weeks.

POTTED HAM

Makes 4 servings

"Potted?" You're probably scratching your head. In Britain, that means something that's a cousin to a pâté, and like pâté, it is served in a small ramekin. Spread this potted ham on pumpernickel or another dark bread.

- ¼ cup chopped cooked British or Canadian bacon (see sidebar, page 91)
- 1 pound cooked ham, roughly chopped
- ¼ cup chopped fresh flat-leaf parsley
- ½ teaspoon ground mace
- ½ teaspoon chili powder
- ½ teaspoon dry mustard powder
- ½ teaspoon freshly ground black pepper
- 4 tablespoons (½ stick) cold unsalted butter, plus 4 tablespoons unsalted butter (optional), melted
- ½ teaspoon salt (optional)
- Pumpernickel or another dark, crusty bread, for serving

1. Combine the bacon, ham, parsley, mace, chili, mustard, and pepper with the cold butter in a food processor or meat grinder. Process or grind the mixture into a puree. Taste the mixture, and add the salt only if it needs it. For a sandwich filling or to spread on bread, serve the potted ham as is, at room temperature.

2. To serve as a dish that will be eaten straight up, spoon the mixture into individual ramekins and pour the melted butter over the tops. Chill in the refrigerator until the butter solidifies, about 1 hour, and serve cold with the bread.

Scotch Eggs

Makes 6 eggs, to serve 3

When I told my wife that I was going to do a book on British food, she demanded that I include Scotch eggs. At first I was put off; I knew them only from chip shops. But when I made them at home, they took on a different character—rich, meaty, and unctuous, rather than greasy. I realized that Scotch eggs needed to be rescued.

1 pound mild bulk sausage
½ teaspoon dried thyme
¼ teaspoon ground mace
1 teaspoon salt
½ teaspoon freshly ground black pepper
6 hard-cooked eggs, peeled
1 cup dried, unflavored bread crumbs
Oil for deep-frying

1. Mix the sausage meat, thyme, mace, salt, and pepper together in a bowl, making sure all the seasonings are distributed well.

2. Divide the meat into 6 equal portions. Place a portion between 2 sheets of parchment or wax paper and roll it with a rolling pin into a rectangle about ¼ inch thick. Repeat with the remaining portions.

3. Wrap each egg with a rectangle of meat, making sure no egg is showing. Put the bread crumbs in a shallow dish, and dredge the eggs in the bread crumbs until they are completely coated.

4. Pour about 6 inches of oil into a heavy pot and heat to 375°F. Fry the eggs, giving them an occasional turn, until the bread crumb crust is well browned, about 3 minutes. Drain on paper towels or a rack. Serve warm.

VARIATION: Instead of frying the eggs, put them on a well-oiled baking sheet and bake at 425°F, turning several times, for about 20 minutes, or until the crust is browned.

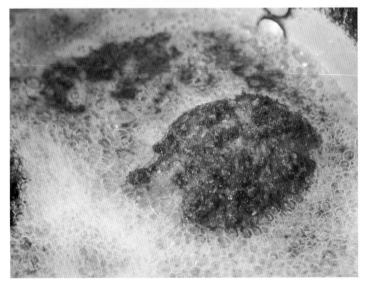

SALMAGUNDI

Makes 4 main-course servings

The ploughman's lunch (see sidebar, page 25) is not the only salad platter in the British repertoire. Not by a long shot. Salmagundi is another classic, a platter of cold dressed meats and vegetables that goes perfectly with a great beer. It's a good way to use one of those rotisserie chickens from the supermarket or take-out store. And the name? It's a corruption of the French word *salmigondis*, which means "hodgepodge."

1 whole roast chicken, cut into serving pieces
4 hard-cooked eggs, peeled and halved lengthwise
4 ounces cooked ham, cut into strips (about 1 cup)
10 anchovy fillets, chopped
1 cup chopped celery
½ cup chopped fresh flat-leaf parsley
1 cup grapes
1 cup cherry tomatoes
½ cup sliced radishes
¼ cup chopped scallion (green part only)
2 tablespoons extra-virgin olive oil
1 tablespoon fresh lemon juice
½ cup pitted olives (optional)
½ cup pickled onions (optional)
Chutney, for serving (Fruit Chutney, page 195, is perfect here)
Rolls, for serving

1. Arrange the chicken pieces and egg halves in a ring around the edge of a large serving platter.

2. Toss together the ham, anchovies, celery, parsley, grapes, tomatoes, radishes, olive oil, lemon juice, and, if you like, the olives and pickled onions, in a large bowl. Make sure all the ingredients are evenly distributed.

3. Mound the ham mixture in the center of the platter. Serve with chutney and rolls on the side.

POTTED ASPARAGUS

Makes 4 servings

Did you think that only meats and seafood could be potted? Asparagus, that favorite of spring vegetables, takes the potting treatment wonderfully. It's a perfect vegetarian substitute for a meat or seafood sandwich spread.

> 4 cups chopped trimmed asparagus (about 1 pound)
> 1 teaspoon salt
> ½ teaspoon freshly ground black pepper
> 2 tablespoons chopped fresh dill
> ¼ cup chopped fresh flat-leaf parsley
> 1 tablespoon chopped fresh chives
> 8 tablespoons (1 stick) unsalted butter, melted

1. Put the asparagus in a microwave-safe bowl, sprinkle with the salt and pepper, and microwave on high until the asparagus is very tender, about 4 minutes.

2. Toss the hot asparagus with the dill, parsley, chives, and 4 tablespoons of the butter. Puree in a food processor until you have a thick paste. Divide the mixture among 4 small ramekins.

3. Cover with the remaining 4 tablespoons of butter and chill for at least 1 hour. Serve cool with bread and grated horseradish. Fish eaters can top potted asparagus with anchovies or Gentleman's Relish (page 193).

a gentleman's secret weapon: the anchovy

When you first start eating traditional English comfort food, you're overwhelmed by the blandness of it all. But pretty soon you discover the sauces. HP Sauce is a spicier, and more tart version of ketchup. And curry sauce, only vaguely related to anything Asian, is found in every snack and sandwich shop. That isn't the end of it, though. There is a whole range of secret weapons in the British kitchen arsenal designed to introduce strong flavors at the right moment. One of the most surprising of all is anchovies.

Anchovies find their way into English cooking in many dishes—in Salmagundi (page 30) and other salads, as an ingredient in the Italian and Spanish dishes people love so much in England, and, finally, in sauces like Gentleman's Relish (page 193). This relish can turn up anywhere—on the jam table at a British bed-and-breakfast, as an ingredient in older recipes, or at British specialty shops. It's like Thai fish sauce, but in a thick paste. Anchovy fans (and you know who you are) shouldn't pass up the chance to try it.

pilgrimage: staffordshire oatcakes

When I decided to turn my attention to Staffordshire oatcakes, the burrito-like filled crêpes from the City of Stoke-on-Trent, I had a plan. It was not a big or ambitious plan. I was just going to approach people in Stoke and ask them cold, "Where might I find a good Staffordshire oatcake?" If someone obviously foreign approached New Yorkers on the street and asked where to find their favorite bagels, or if people in Naples were quizzed about their favorite pizza shop, the excitement would be palpable.

The good citizens of Stoke were excited, too, just for a different reason. They were thrilled to tell me that all the oatcake shops were closed. A visit to the tourist information office confirmed what I had gleaned. They insisted that oatcake shops were open only on certain mornings, and that I could never find them anyway.

Undeterred, I continued my quest on my own. Stoke turned out to be doing a lousy job of keeping its secrets. Within a few minutes' walk of the tourist office was an outdoor oatcake stand run by an enthusiastic couple. I ordered an oatcake filled with bacon and mushrooms, stood in the drizzle, and watched them make it. The "cake" itself was made with a thin batter, and the filling was grilled separately. I followed it with a second course, an oatcake filled with cheese and onions. The proprietors took a prepared oatcake, put it back on the grill to reheat it, smothered it with some grated cheddar and raw onion, and let it fry until the cheese melted. Then they rolled it into a tube, much like a burrito, and rolled the tube with white deli paper. There was lots of texture from the just barely cooked onions, some deep notes from the oats, and plenty of savor (and grease) from the grill.

A few minutes later I stopped in at a nearby café, where I noticed they, too, served oatcakes—and nobody was eating them. This time I split the difference and chose cheese and mushroom. Instead of being rolled, the oatcakes at this café were just folded, with the filling in the middle. (This turned out to be the norm, I eventually learned.) It made for a nicer plate, but the rich and oat-y flavor was the same.

At that point, I was stuffed. But I resolved to return to Stoke again on a day when the oatcake shops were open, in order to find out more. That day came three months later. I had all my ducks in a row: a (horrible)

room in town booked for Friday and Saturday night, a street map with the locations of oatcake shops marked about as accurately as I was able to, and printouts from several oatcake fan sites.

Morning arrived bright with sunshine. I brought forth every last bit of self-control and had only toast and coffee for breakfast. I planned to do lots of eating later. I didn't walk more than a hundred yards from my room before I came to my first oatcake shop. It was a classic small-scale professional food service: four people crammed into a space about six feet square, each doing what amounted to a choreographed dance routine in order to stay on top of demand. Up front the crowds were two and three deep, anxiously waiting for their cakes while more and more went on the grill.

Strolling from oatcake shop to oatcake shop, I soon caught on to the routine. You could tell where the shops were from the people (and strollers and shopping carts) lined up outside and the cars double- and triple-parked in front. A typical transaction went something like this:

"Hello Richard, what can I get for you today?"

"Three cheese, egg, and bacon please, and two dozen plain."

"Fine. Is Claire still sleeping with her dentist?"

"She is, and make that three dozen."

No transaction went without an exchange of gossip, and very few people ate just one oatcake. Every place had its fans, and every fan wanted to talk oatcakes with me. Each directed me to another shop. Eventually I approached one with no crowd out front. It was afternoon and time to close. Did Stoke have another unknown, unsung specialty food for evenings? I asked the question a hundred different ways and no was the only answer. If you're too late for oatcakes, you get fish and chips or balti (see sidebar, page 104), the same as every place else.

At the end of the day, I had a pretty good idea of what

oatcakes were all about. The crêpes had to be rich, oat-y, almost yeasty, and tender in the center (like an Ethiopian *injera*, if you have had one of those), but crisp at the edges.

Were some shops better than others? Not really. There were differences, but the similarities outweighed them. Consistent were the claims that everybody's shop was the best, and that the recipe was a tightly guarded secret. I made the mistake of laughing at one person who told me this. "You'll never guess what's in them!" he declared. "Well, oat flour, wheat flour, and yeast for starters," I said. While he stared in

amazement, I changed the subject and simply told him, "Your oatcakes are the best I've tasted."

Staffordshire oatcakes are unsung heroes of regional British cooking. There's no better way to eat oats than this. My fellow oatcake fans boasted that "even 20 miles away, nobody knows what these things are." How true. The tourism industry has missed the boat here; they should be promoting Stoke worldwide as the city that wakes to delicious whole-grain crêpes—on certain days.

My own favorite? Cheese and mushroom. But they aren't bad plain either.

Stoke-on-Trent, England

STAFFORDSHIRE OATCAKES

Makes 8 oatcakes, to serve 4

While I prefer my oatcakes plain, almost anything that can go into a full breakfast can be stuffed into an oatcake: bacon, sausage, mushroom, and onion are all fine. Whatever you choose, it will taste best with melted cheddar cheese. You'll find oat flour in health food stores, and you can also order it online.

2 cups oat flour
2 cups all-purpose flour
1 teaspoon salt
1 packet instant yeast (about 2¼ teaspoons)
1 cup whole milk, at room temperature
3 cups water

FILLINGS
1 cup shredded cheddar cheese
3 slices cooked British bacon (see sidebar, page 91)
1 cup cooked sausage
1 cup sliced sautéed mushroom
1 cup chopped onion

1. Sift the oat flour, all-purpose flour, salt, and instant yeast together into a large bowl. Add the milk and water and stir to make a thin, smooth batter with no lumps. If the batter is too thick, add more water, 1 tablespoon at time, until you have an easily poured liquid batter, rather than a dough. Set the batter aside at room temperature for 1 hour. If it is going to stand longer, refrigerate it, covered, for up to 24 hours.

2. Put a well-oiled skillet or flat griddle on high heat. Ladle about ½ cup of batter into the skillet so it forms a thin pancake. Let the batter cook undisturbed until bubbles form on the surface and the bottom is browned, about 2 minutes, and then flip the oatcake with a spatula. Cook until the oatcake is browned on the other side, about 2 minutes more.

3. Remove the oatcake from the pan and put it on a plate. Place your choice of fillings on one side of the oatcake and fold the other end over like a soft taco. If you are using shredded cheese and move quickly, there should be enough heat to start it melting; otherwise, a few seconds in the microwave should take care of it. Serve it right away.

4. Repeat with the remaining batter and filling. If you're making a batch of oatcakes for a large group, hold them for up to 30 minutes in a warm oven. Store leftover oatcakes in the refrigerator. (Oatcake fanatics will eat them cold; the rest of us reheat them.)

SALMON *and* CUCUMBER SANDWICH

Makes 4 sandwiches, to serve 4

"What could be so difficult about making a sandwich?" you ask. Well, if they're so easy to make, how come they often seem to ooze salty, watery, yucky stuff? There's room for improvement, isn't there? To get the cucumber slices quite thin, use a mandoline if you have one. The slices should be so thin that they are not crunchy to the bite.

Should you cut the crusts off? It makes for a more elegant presentation, but if your bread is good, you're throwing something delicious away.

1 cup thinly sliced seedless cucumber
1 teaspoon salt
1 (7½-ounce) can red salmon
1 tablespoon olive oil
1 tablespoon fresh lemon juice
1 teaspoon freshly ground white pepper
8 slices fine-grained white or whole-wheat bread
2 tablespoons unsalted butter, at room temperature

1. Put the cucumber slices in a colander and sprinkle them with the salt. Let them drain for at least 30 minutes.

2. Combine the salmon, olive oil, lemon juice, and pepper in a bowl. Mash the salmon with a fork, and toss until the lemon and oil are evenly distributed.

3. Spread 4 of the bread slices with the butter. Top with a thin layer of the dressed salmon, and cover with cucumber slices. Put the remaining slices of bread on top to make sandwiches, and then cut the sandwiches in half diagonally. Serve quickly; the salting and draining help, but any delay courts trouble.

DEVILED CRAB

Makes 4 servings

This British cousin of the crab cake is a great choice when you're looking for a seafood dish that isn't fried. While it's true that American blue or king crabs are a bit different from the brown crabs caught in the UK, any crabmeat will do the job.

- **4 tablespoons (½ stick) unsalted butter, melted**
- **1 cup dried, unflavored bread crumbs**
- **2 teaspoons mild curry paste**
- **1 teaspoon Worcestershire sauce**
- **2 tablespoons heavy cream**
- **1 pound lump crabmeat**
- **4 lemon slices**

1. Combine 2 tablespoons of the butter and ½ cup of the bread crumbs with the curry paste, Worcestershire sauce, cream, and crabmeat in a large bowl. Stir well to distribute the ingredients evenly.

2. In a small bowl, mix the remaining 2 tablespoons butter and ½ cup bread crumbs together. There should be no lumps.

3. Divide the crabmeat mixture into 4 parts and put each in an ovenproof ramekin. Top each with a quarter of the butter–bread crumb mixture.

4. Position a rack 6 inches from the heat source of your broiler, and preheat the broiler on low. Broil until the bread crumb topping is deeply browned but not burned, about 8 minutes. Serve immediately.

pilgrimage: brooklyn and the fine art of frying

I don't know if there's an official count of the world cuisines you can sample in New York City's restaurants. Over the years, I've eaten the foods of Argentina, Brazil, Cambodia, China, Colombia, Cuba, Georgia, Germany, Greece, Honduras, Hungary, Italy, Japan, Korea, Mexico, Peru, Poland, Portugal, Russia, Spain, Sri Lanka, Tajikistan, Thailand, Ukraine, Uruguay, and Uzbekistan. But British is another story. I recall being taken to an authentic tea room once. But only in the last few years have there been enough British restaurants to attract some notice.

One day I headed over to the Park Slope Chipshop, one of the city's outposts of traditional British cooking. It's a few minutes by train from Manhattan on Fifth Avenue in Brooklyn's Park Slope. What I expected was a typical take-out place with stainless-steel counters and vats of frying oil within ten feet of the cash register. Instead, I was pleasantly surprised to find one of my favorite kinds of British restaurants, a real sit-down fish-and-chips place.

Inside there were tables, chairs, and Union Jacks. The walls were decorated with artwork that screamed "Great Britain!" From where I sat, a picture of the queen stared down at me, and possibly a few Beatles portraits, too.

Although fish-and-chip classics were on the menu, it was actually more Scottish than English, with haggis and the whole range of deep-fried

Scottish favorites. Indeed, deep-fried macaroni and cheese was on the specials board, along with a twice-fried cherry pie.

I sat down with Chris Sell, the very British founder and owner, to discuss Americans' relationship with British food, and what foods expat Brits miss the most. "I wanted to be absolutely traditional," Chris said. "I didn't want to put anything American on the menu at all." It turned out, though, that our definitions of American were different. Yes, Chris thought of his deep-fried Twinkies as American because, well, Twinkies were. The logic was there, but his Twinkies were so rooted in the Scottish culture of snack-frying that it was a tough argument.

Chris has accomplished quite a bit here. As the first Twinkie fryer in the United States, he's been the subject of both a Trivial Pursuit and a *Jeopardy!* question. This has given Chris the impression that deep-fried macaroni and cheese and deep-fried pizza are foods that Americans crave more than people in the British Isles do. He told me people who order the "trifecta of death," his phrase for his biggest selling fried items, are almost certainly going to be Americans.

The Chipshop attracts a mixed crowd. Expats come in for bangers and mash, local Anglophiles for fish and chips, tourists for the fried items, and everybody for shepherd's pie. Of course, English beers are popular across the board.

Our conversation turned to the difference between British chips and American fries. First Chris went on a rant about fries formed from textured, processed ingredients. He insisted that a major fast-food chain made them this way instead of using whole, real potatoes, and the entire nation followed its example. It was the sort of broad—and completely mistaken—brush that should have upset me but instead made me chuckle a bit.

Here's his version of the distinction: Fries, he says, are from the French culinary tradition. The potatoes are thinly sliced and fried until they're very crisp. Chips are larger—Chris tells me his are 14 millimeters (about ½ inch) thick, and are fried just until the potato is cooked through. When asked why chips have to be so tender, he answered with the obvious, "to soak up vinegar, of course!"

With that, I turned to the Chipshop menu and was overpowered by a sort of strange magnetic pull toward the fryer. Instead of the fish and chips and mushy peas I intended to order, I polished off two slices of deep-fried pizza and a whole ball of deep-fried macaroni and cheese. For a couple of hours after my meal, I basked in its unctuous deliciousness, and then spent the next three days sick to my stomach. Within a day of feeling better, I was already planning a return trip.

The
SOUP POT

In Scotland, soup is everywhere you turn, and there are dozens of words to describe it. *Bree* (page 56) and *skink* (page 57), to cite two examples from this chapter, are just the beginning.

While people all over Britain eat soup, it's consumed with the greatest gusto in Scotland, where a wide range of traditional broths, often thick soups despite the name, are a mainstay. It's all too easy to imagine: the wind howling, the rain pounding, a pantry filled with barley, leeks, and lamb. In the world of British food, Scotland is the home of soup, where most of the legendary recipes come from, where it's most often consumed, and where you'll most want a bowl.

BEEF TEA

Makes 2 servings

Beef "tea?" Is that like beef broth? Well, kind of. It's a dish that goes back in time to the days when the British were trying to find the essence of what gave beef its nutritional value. Since this was before vitamins and protein were known, they weren't sure what they were looking for. Along the way, somebody noticed that this very mild liquid was soothing and comforting. Give it a try when you're feeling under the weather, but don't go looking for a scientific reason for its effectiveness.

For steeping the "tea," you will need a 1-quart wide-mouth glass jar or plastic container with a tight-fitting lid.

8 ounces beef chuck steak, cut into ½-inch cubes
¼ teaspoon salt
3 cups water

1. Combine the beef, salt, and water in a saucepan and bring to a boil over high heat. Let the mixture boil for 1 minute. Reduce the heat to low and let the water barely simmer for 20 minutes more, skimming off any scum that forms on the surface. Remove the pan from the heat and let cool.

2. Pour the liquid and the pieces of beef into the jar or container, cover it tightly, and let the liquid steep (like tea, of course) in the refrigerator for at least 24 hours.

3. Strain the liquid through either cheesecloth or a fine-mesh strainer and discard the beef. You'll be left with the tea. Serve hot.

Scotch Broth: Lamb *and* Barley Soup

Makes 6 servings

Yet another one of those "broths" that's really best described as a stew, this is the soup that expresses the Scottish harvest perfectly. Cook it on a cold afternoon and warm your house up the traditional way. Enjoy the barley, lamb, and split peas, all classic crops of the British Isles. It's a history lesson in a bowl.

1 cup pearl barley
¼ cup dried split peas
1 pound lamb stew meat, cut into 1-inch cubes
1 cup chopped onion
8 cups water
1 cup chopped leek
1 cup chopped turnip
2 cups chopped fresh kale (preferable) or 1 cup frozen
    chopped kale
1 tablespoon Worcestershire sauce
1 teaspoon freshly ground black pepper
2 teaspoons salt

1. Combine the barley, split peas, lamb, onion, and water in a large soup pot. Bring to a boil over high heat, and let the broth boil for 1 minute. Reduce the heat and simmer the soup, covered, stirring occasionally, for 1 hour or until the barley starts to soften.

2. Stir in the leeks and turnips. Cook at a simmer for 30 minutes more, or until the turnips are very tender.

3. Add the kale, Worcestershire sauce, pepper, and salt and continue simmering the soup until the kale is tender, about 15 minutes. Serve hot.

COCK-A-LEEKIE: CHICKEN, LEEK, *and* PRUNE SOUP

Makes 6 servings

To really understand this dish, you have to imagine a time centuries ago when dried fruits were exotic ingredients and a badge of wealth and sophistication. If you're wondering if there's anything in the name, well, not really. It's just a jumble of Old English and Scottish Gaelic—a reminder that the original ingredients were a cock ready for the soup pot and some leeks.

2 pounds chicken thighs
2 cups chopped leek
½ cup chopped carrot
½ cup chopped celery
¼ cup pearl barley
1 bay leaf
2 cloves
2 cups whole milk
8 cups water
1 cup halved pitted prunes
1 teaspoon salt
1 teaspoon freshly ground black pepper

1. Combine the chicken, leek, carrot, celery, barley, bay leaf, cloves, milk, and water in a large soup pot over medium heat. Bring the broth to a simmer and let the broth cook, uncovered, stirring occasionally, until the chicken is cooked all the way through, about 1½ hours. Remove the chicken from the pot and let the meat cool. Keep the soup at a simmer.

2. Remove the chicken meat from the bones and return the meat to the soup. Discard the bones.

3. Add the prunes, salt, and pepper and continue to simmer the soup until the liquid has reduced by a third and the flavors are well combined, about 1 hour more. Remove the bay leaf and serve hot.

CREAM of WATERCRESS SOUP

Makes 4 servings

Watercress, that most British of greens, can do more than perk up a salad or sit under a slather of mayo in a sandwich. Its distinctive flavor is delicious in soup.

> 1 tablespoon unsalted butter
> 1 cup chopped onion
> 2 cups watercress, stems trimmed
> 4 cups low-sodium chicken broth
> ¼ cup heavy cream
> ½ teaspoon salt

1. Melt the butter in a saucepan over medium-low heat. Add the onion and cook, stirring occasionally, until it is tender and translucent, about 15 minutes.

2. Stir in the watercress and continue cooking, stirring occasionally, until it has completely wilted, about 2 minutes. Remove the pan from the heat.

3. Transfer to a blender or food processor and puree into a smooth liquid.

4. Pour the liquid into a soup pot and bring to a simmer over medium-low heat. Mix in the cream. It's important to keep the heat down here. If you let it come to a boil, you'll have a broken-up mess.

5. Taste the soup and, if it needs the salt, add it. Otherwise, it's ready for serving. Serve hot.

SCOTCH OATMEAL SOUP

Makes 4 servings

We're so used to eating oatmeal as a morning cereal that we kind of forget that it has other uses. How about in a soup, so it can warm you up in the evening the same way it does at breakfast?

1 tablespoon peanut oil
1 cup chopped carrot
1 cup chopped leek
1 cup chopped onion
2 cups ½-inch-wide green cabbage strips
2 cups canned crushed tomatoes
2 cups low-sodium chicken broth
2 cups whole milk
⅓ cup rolled oats (not instant)
½ teaspoon salt

1. Put the oil, carrot, leek, onion, and cabbage in a large soup pot over medium heat and cook, stirring frequently, until the cabbage and onion are translucent and beginning to brown at the edges, about 20 minutes.

2. Mix in the tomato, broth, milk, oats, and salt; reduce the heat so the soup is simmering; and continue to cook, stirring occasionally, until the oats and vegetables are completely cooked and the liquid has reduced by a quarter, about 40 minutes. Serve hot.

Salmon Broth

Makes 4 servings

Sometimes I wonder if there's a bit of irony in the custom of calling some hearty Scottish soups broths. In no way could this be reconstituted from a cube or poured out of a carton. Salmon broth is really a meal in itself. In fine restaurants it's a first course, but in a local pub, it might be served as the main dish.

> 1 pound salmon fillet, cut into 1-inch squares
> 2 sprigs fresh thyme
> 2 sprigs fresh flat-leaf parsley, plus 1 teaspoon chopped fresh parsley, for garnish
> 1 tablespoon chopped fresh chives
> 4 cups water
> 1 cup peeled pearl onions
> 1 cup chopped carrot
> 1 cup chopped potato
> 2 tablespoons unsalted butter
> 1 cup heavy cream
> 2 teaspoons salt

1. Combine the salmon, thyme, parsley, chives, and water in a large soup pot over high heat. Bring to a boil and let boil, uncovered, for 1 minute. Reduce the heat to medium-low and simmer the soup, covered, stirring occasionally, for 5 minutes, or until the salmon is opaque.

2. Add the onions, carrot, potato, butter, and cream and simmer, uncovered, until the potatoes and carrots are tender and the liquid has reduced by about a quarter, about 40 minutes.

3. Taste the soup and, if it needs salt, first add just 1 teaspoon. Then taste again to see if it needs more. It's all too easy to make soups like this one too salty.

4. Remove the sprigs of thyme and parsley. Garnish with the chopped parsley, and serve hot.

MULLIGATAWNY SOUP

Makes 4 servings

At one time, this soup was enjoyed in England as an example of authentic regional Indian cooking, and Tamil cooks make a traditional version today. However, decades of comingling with other ingredients in the kitchens of the soup-loving British have morphed it into something that's only barely recognizable as South Asian.

2 tablespoons unsalted butter

1 tablespoon mild curry paste

¼ teaspoon ground nutmeg

1 cup chopped onion

1 cup chopped apple

½ cup chopped carrot

½ cup chopped red bell pepper

4 cups low-sodium chicken broth

½ pound boneless, skinless chicken breast, cut into thumbnail-size pieces

½ teaspoon salt

¼ teaspoon freshly ground black pepper

½ cup heavy cream

1. Melt the butter in a soup pot over medium heat, add the curry paste, and stir until they're well combined.

2. Add the nutmeg, onion, apple, carrot, and bell pepper and continue cooking, stirring occasionally, until the onion is translucent and the pepper is fork tender, about 10 minutes.

3. Mix in the chicken broth, bring to a boil, and continue boiling for 1 minute. Then turn off the heat.

4. Use an immersion blender to create a puree from the curry-vegetable mixture.

5. Return the mixture to medium heat and add the chicken, salt, black pepper, and cream. Allow it to simmer, uncovered, for about 30 minutes or until the chicken is fully cooked. Serve hot.

Lincoln Cathedral, England

pilgrimage: **away from it all**

I was on Rousay. It's an outlying island in the Orkney chain and pretty far north of just about everything. The nearest real town—itself on a tiny island called Orkney Mainland—is a half-hour ferry ride plus a half-hour bus ride away. And to get to the solid ground of Scotland, you face a couple of buses on Mainland, and then a 90-minute boat ride due south. Get off that boat, and you'll be almost in Thurso, a six-hour train ride from Aberdeen or Glasgow. Rousay is a pretty remote place.

Why did I come here? To find out if some sort of "real" Scotland exists in its rural and less visited corners. Would Rousay be a true *Brigadoon,* a Scotland unsullied by fast-food chains, gossip magazines, and deep frying?

When I stepped off the ferry on an early Saturday evening, the combination store-pub-restaurant at the Rousay pier was buzzing. Soon I had a pickled egg, a plate of fish and chips, and a shot of whisky in front of me and was chatting with the crowd. And you could tell what kind of crowd it was. The moment I asked if they had Wi-Fi, one of the patrons left the bar, ran to the back, and came out with all the pieces needed to assemble a public Wi-Fi system (still in the box). Soon they were assembling away.

It wasn't long before people were quarreling with each other over the right to drive me to the farm-hostel. (It was less than three hundred yards away, but I didn't know that yet.) I chose the most sober among them, and moments later I was dropped off.

Before I even noticed the place, there was its location—just a couple of green fields separated it from the sea. It wasn't open ocean, though. I could see Egilsay and other islands in the Orkney chain. The hostel was a surprisingly suburban-looking modern house, which stood a few yards from a traditional farm, with grazing animals and all.

Eric, the farmer, greeted me with a question about the New York Dolls, a band I routinely confuse with the Sex Pistols. I did not hold my own in this conversation, and a nasty rain and biting wind kept me from wandering off and exploring the area.

I decided to hit the road and see the island. Since there are only 14 miles of road here, that wasn't much

of a task. First I grabbed a bowl of one of those broth soups at the island's other pub. At this point, I was starting to get used to the friendliness of the residents and was soon listening to the bartender's life story. After I finished my soup and checked my email— this place had its wireless Internet hooked up—the bartender offered me eggs from her hens to cook at the hostel, so I wouldn't have to walk back for supper. I did do some walking, though. First I stopped to look at some ancient tombs, which the island folks call cairns. They have chambers that look like root cellars, and these are the biggest clue to what Rousay life was like thousands of years ago.

While I was pondering this, I found myself face to face with the islands' relentless friendliness once again. This time, a salmon farmer offered to take me on a tour. Hoping for some insight into traditional life, I hopped into his beat-up old Land Rover. There were rolling meadows filled with grazing cows and sheep, a bit of vegetable farming, and those typical Scots country houses with chimneys at either end. What

was totally absent was any sign of commercial activity. I knew the island had two pubs, a hostel, a store, a gym, and at least one B & B, but the signs for them were discreet.

I skipped the gym (yeah, I know, don't remind me) and headed for the store. It was not on the main loop road and was open only at certain times (2:00 to 4:00 p.m. on Sundays, for example). The tiny store had both everything and nothing, depending on your perspective. There were simmer sauces for making quick curries; the ingredients for traditional home cooking, like flour and smoked herring; the usual sweets and soft drinks; and a selection of single malt whiskies that would please many connoisseurs.

More than for its inventory, the shop was for sociability. The owner engaged everybody who came in with cheerful banter, and outside at the gas pump, there were so many people and so much talk that it was a real party.

On the ferry back, I fell into a conversation with a woman who grew up in Glasgow and was working as an air-traffic controller at the Orkney airport. When I asked her what she liked about living on Orkney, she shrugged. But when we talked about what she missed, her eyes became dreamy as she described the joys of that great Glasgow specialty, deep-fried pizza. "They dip the pizza in batter and fry it; it's so lovely!" she told me.

There's nothing like that in the Orkney.

CAWL CENNIN: WELSH-STYLE LEEK *and* POTATO SOUP
Makes 4 servings

On March 1, Wales celebrates a holiday for David, its patron saint, with a bowl of soup made from its favorite vegetable: the leek. Few Americans may celebrate St. David's Day, but when leeks are in season, it's a great soup to make anyway.

4 cups low-sodium chicken broth
1 cup chopped British or Canadian bacon (see sidebar, page 91)
2 cups chopped potato
3 cups chopped leek
1 cup whole milk
½ teaspoon freshly ground black pepper
1 tablespoon finely chopped fresh flat-leaf parsley (optional)

1. Bring the chicken broth to a simmer in a large soup pot over medium heat. Add the bacon, potato, and leek and cook, covered, stirring occasionally, until the potatoes are fork tender, about 40 minutes.

2. Use a skimmer to remove the solids from the broth. Put them in a bowl and use a potato masher to break them down. They need a bit of work, but you don't want a real puree.

3. Return the mashed vegetables to the broth and add the milk and pepper. Simmer, uncovered, over medium heat for 20 minutes, or until the soup has reduced by about a quarter.

4. If you like, sprinkle with the parsley just before serving. Serve hot.

PARTAN BREE: SCOTTISH CREAM *of* CRAB SOUP

Makes 4 servings

Not exactly a chowder, *partan bree* is a classic soup from Scotland. *Partan* is Scottish Gaelic for "crab." And *bree*? No, it's not the soft French cheese; it's like our word "brew."

3 cups fish broth
3 anchovy fillets, chopped
½ cup white rice
2 cups whole milk
8 ounces crabmeat (see Note)
1 teaspoon salt
½ teaspoon freshly ground white pepper
¼ cup heavy cream
2 tablespoons chopped fresh flat-leaf parsley

1. Combine the broth, anchovy fillets, and rice in a soup pot and bring to a boil over high heat. Let the liquid boil for 1 minute, reduce the heat to medium-low, and add the milk. Simmer, covered, until the rice is very tender, about 25 minutes. Remove from the heat.

2. Mix in the crabmeat, salt, pepper, and cream and puree the soup in a food processor or directly in the pot with an immersion blender.

3. Return the pureed soup to the pot if you used a food processor, and warm on medium-low heat until it's hot enough to serve. Ladle into bowls and sprinkle with the chopped parsley. Serve hot.

NOTE: The soup works with frozen, pasteurized, or even canned crabmeat.

CULLEN SKINK: SMOKED HADDOCK *and* POTATO SOUP

Makes 4 servings

The flavor of smoke in a soup! This is the dish that smoked-food fans like myself have been searching for. Wondering what *cullen* *skink* means? Cullen is a seaside town east of Inverness, on the Scottish north coast, and *skink* is a local word for soup or broth.

- **1 pound smoked haddock fillets**
- **4 cups water**
- **1 bay leaf**
- **1 cup chopped onion**
- **1 cup mashed potato**
- **1 cup whole milk**
- **2 tablespoons unsalted butter**
- **½ teaspoon salt**
- **½ teaspoon freshly ground white pepper**
- **2 tablespoons chopped fresh flat-leaf parsley**

1. Put the haddock in a large soup pot and add the water. Place over high heat, bring to a boil, and let the fish continue boiling for 1 minute.

2. Reduce the heat to medium-low, cover, and simmer for another 15 minutes. Give the soup a few brisk stirs to break the fish up into flakes.

3. Add the bay leaf, onion, and potato. Simmer the soup, covered, stirring occasionally, for 15 minutes more.

4. Mix in the milk and butter and taste the soup. If it needs the salt, add it, and then sprinkle in the pepper. Simmer until the milk has warmed through and combined with the other flavors, about 5 minutes. Remove the bay leaf and serve warm, topped with chopped parsley.

The
MAIN COURSE

I t's the plate of food that you order at the bar, it's what they bring you at a sit-down fish-and-chips restaurant, and it may even be lunch at a tea or coffee shop. These dishes, "mains" in British parlance, are what most of us want when we're thinking about a meal.

The recipes that follow run from the modest Dumplings and Mince (page 67) to showpieces like Beef Wellington (page 63). They're as familiar as Classic Roast Beef with Gravy (page 68) and as surprising as Lamb's Tongue with Raisin Sauce (page 95). All are worth a try.

pilgrimage: haggis

No food actually eaten in the Western world frightens people the way haggis does. I used to say that haggis is just like scrapple, but it didn't take long for me to realize that this comforted nobody. Why is this simple, traditional food so scary? How can it affect people that deeply? And just what is haggis, anyway?

Haggis is a large, well-seasoned sausage made from the organ meats of sheep. It's in the same family as liverwurst, kishke, boudin, and even mortadella. Some people claim that this is the most Scottish of foods, but similar items are served all over Europe, and there's plenty of evidence that it was brought to Scotland by the Vikings.

Most haggis produced today is packed in artificial casings, making it appear strangely hot dog–like. A proper haggis, however, is stuffed in a sheep's stomach and has that aura of a quality artisanal sausage about it. Seasoning is an issue, too. Commercial haggis is a bit

too toned down, while the real thing is more distinctively flavored. It doesn't have the garlic-heavy taste of its European cousins but instead has hints of pepper, nutmeg, and mace, which complement its basic richness.

In northern England and in Scotland, haggis is typically fried and served with chips, or it's sliced, grilled, and put in a sandwich. Better, though, is a whole poached haggis. You can scoop out the insides and have yourself a good pâté. Or do as serious Scottish chefs do and use it as a filling or stuffing for a chicken breast.

In the States and in Scotland, too, the big time for haggis consumption is Robert Burns Night, which is January 25, the birthday of the Scottish poet Robert Burns. You may have seen the celebrations on videos. People put on their kilts and tartans and gather in groups in order to drink whisky, eat haggis, and listen to bagpipe music. The traditional Burns Night meal calls for a serving of haggis with sides of

potatoes and rutabagas. (I know, rutabagas are another "everybody hates them" sort of food.)

I have to confess that before I began writing this book, my experience with haggis was not extensive. I had eaten the battered and fried version maybe three times at chip shops, and a grilled haggis sandwich exactly once, all in Britain. Never had I tried what one sees on (almost always American) Internet videos—a football-sized oval of grainy meat presented by a guy in a kilt who's being followed by bagpipers.

A call to a well-known Scottish restaurant in my home state of New Jersey didn't quite work out the way I wanted it to. When the guy who answered the phone suggested I have a seafood pasta instead, I cried a few quiet tears. I had better luck with the place down the street, which offered "Robert Burns dinners" of haggis, potatoes, and turnips—the latter two known as *tatties* and *neeps* in the local jargon—every Friday and Saturday in January. When I asked on the phone how much a Robert Burns dinner would cost, I was told "two pounds for twenty-five dollars." Sadly, it was too late to drive over that evening, because I found a two-pound order of steaming haggis to be intriguing.

I hopped in my car the next day and headed over to the restaurant, which was in the town of Kearny. When I arrived, I found something unexpected: a nice, clean, Brazilian-Portuguese neighborhood with a couple of old Scottish storefronts mixed in. No wonder seafood pasta was popular!

I took a seat and started eavesdropping on the other customers. All were talking

haggis and none were ordering it. When the guy at the table behind me called it a national joke, I could feel my blood pressure going up sharply. Looking around in a vain attempt to gain my composure, I realized that the place was too Scottish to actually *be* Scottish. There were prints of guys in kilts playing bagpipes and portraits of Robert Burns. No posters of football teams, no adverts for fizzy drinks. It was a fantasy of Scotland rather than the real thing.

I ordered haggis, and that's what I got. On my plate was the kind of fried haggis that one is served in chip shops pretty much anywhere north of Manchester, along with ramekins of mashed rutabagas and potatoes. All were quite good, but I wanted at least a slice of that football of grainy meat.

I strolled down the street, passing one nice-looking Portuguese joint after another, until I reached a place called Stewart's of Kearny. This small butcher shop had a price board listing

items like black pudding, white pudding, and, I was glad to see, haggis. I asked for a small haggis and the butcher brought out a real one, an actual animal stomach filled with rich, pink meat. I took a couple of deep breaths and pulled out my credit card.

Back home in my kitchen, I simmered the haggis, fixed up some mashed potatoes and turnips (the rutabagas at my local produce shop looked awful), and dug in. It was nothing like the fried stuff. Instead, it was a smooth, peppery pâté with the sort of rich, meaty unctuousness that people often associate with French food. It was so good that even my wife liked it, a rare compliment for my cooking.

As I cleaned up, I wondered how haggis would be received here if it were Italian or French. Obviously, I reckoned, American food tourists would come back from Europe raving about it, and there would be discussions of how to smuggle it into the States

in one's luggage. Reporters from glossy magazines would go on about the haggis they had in a small-town café that's run by a grandma. It would be revered in the same way that other French and Italian artisanal meat products are. True, that fried one did nothing for the cause, although I know people who would rave if they were served a whole deep-fried salami somewhere in rural Tuscany. But haggis is so forlorn that it needs more than a publicity campaign or fancy label.

"National joke?" No way! It's classic poverty cuisine, in this case a delicious way to preserve the most perishable parts of a newly slaughtered sheep. The joke, I think, is on everybody who won't eat haggis, for whatever reason. It's their loss.

BEEF WELLINGTON

Makes 6 servings

Beef Wellington, a roast beef wrapped in a pastry crust, is named for the First Duke of Wellington. It's an old-school classic, an elegant dish that the British consumed before the phrase "fine dining" was heard everywhere. Today it seems almost corny, but it became a legend for a reason.

1 (2- to 2½-pound) piece beef tenderloin fillet
2 teaspoons salt
1 teaspoon freshly ground black pepper
2 tablespoons vegetable oil
1 tablespoon unsalted butter
1 cup chopped onion
3 cups chopped mushrooms
1 (17½-ounce) package frozen puff pastry, thawed
1 large egg, beaten

1. Preheat the oven to 400°F. Sprinkle the beef tenderloin with 1 teaspoon of the salt and ½ teaspoon of the pepper. Pour the oil in a large skillet over high heat. Add the beef tenderloin and brown it on all sides. (Make sure it is really browned, and not just gray.) Remove the beef to a platter and set it aside to cool. Reserve the drippings and juices in the skillet.

2. Reduce the heat to medium-low and add the butter and onion to the same skillet. Cook, stirring occasionally, until the onion is translucent and has absorbed much of the fat that was rendered when the tenderloin was browned, about 15 minutes.

3. Mix in the mushrooms and the remaining 1 teaspoon of salt and ½ teaspoon of pepper and cook, stirring occasionally, until the mushrooms have completely cooked and the liquid in the pan has thickened into a sauce-like consistency, about 20 minutes. Remove from the heat, set aside, and let cool.

4. Lay a puff pastry sheet down on a flat surface and cut out a rectangle large enough to cover the entire beef tenderloin. Put the beef on the pastry sheet and spread the mushrooms out over the beef. Wrap the pastry around the beef and mushrooms and pinch the dough seam to seal it tightly all the way around. Oil a baking sheet well, transfer the wrapped beef to the sheet, and brush the pastry with the beaten egg.

5. Roast the beef for 45 minutes, or until a meat thermometer reads 130°F and the pastry is browned. Remove from the oven and let cool for 15 minutes. Slice the beef into 1-inch-thick slices, and serve warm. Or chill in the refrigerator and serve cold.

BOILED BEEF

Makes 4 servings

When people first hear about this recipe, they assume it's something like boiled hamburgers. Names can be deceiving, though. *Boiled beef* is just a British name for what Americans would call cooked corned beef or New England boiled dinner. It also goes under the names *salt beef* and *salted beef* in Great Britain. In the UK and Ireland the leftovers are relished in the legendary Bubble and Squeak (page 128). Note that you will soak the corned beef for 6 hours before cooking.

1 (3-pound) corned beef brisket
2 cups chopped carrot
1 cup chopped celery
1 cup chopped turnip
2 cups pearl onions
1 cup sliced leek (white part only)
4 whole cloves
8 whole black peppercorns
2 bay leaves
1 sprig fresh thyme
1 sprig fresh sage
1 sprig fresh rosemary

1. Rinse off the beef brisket in cold water. Soak it in cold water to cover for at least 6 hours in the refrigerator to help remove the surface salt.

2. Drain the beef and place it in a large pot. Add fresh cold water until the meat is just covered. Cover the pot, bring to a simmer over medium heat, and cook, stirring occasionally, until the meat starts to become tender, about 1 hour.

3. Add the carrot, celery, turnip, onions, leek, cloves, peppercorns, bay leaves, thyme, sage, and rosemary to the pot. Simmer, covered, stirring occasionally, until the meat and vegetables are very tender, about 2 hours more.

4. Remove from the heat. Take out and discard the bay leaves, thyme, sage, and rosemary. Serve the warm meat and vegetables together.

BEEF COLLOPS *with* PICKLED WALNUTS

Makes 4 servings

This is really just a simple beef and wine sauce dish—*collop* is just the British word for what the French call *escalope* or the Swedish *kallop*, meaning a small piece of meat—with one very interesting added ingredient, pickled walnuts. They are just that: fresh, green walnuts pickled like vegetables. You can buy them in a jar at any British food shop or website in the United States.

Note that in this recipe you cook the onions and beef mixtures separately, but at the same time.

    2 tablespoons olive oil
    1½ pounds Swiss steak
    5 medium-size onions, 1 chopped (about 1 cup) and 4 sliced
      (about 4 cups)
    ½ teaspoon dried thyme
    ½ teaspoon salt
    ½ teaspoon freshly ground black pepper
    1 cup sliced mushrooms
    ½ cup sliced pickled walnuts
    2 cups red wine

1. Heat 1 tablespoon of the olive oil in a Dutch oven over medium-high heat. Brown the steak pieces well in the olive oil. (Make sure they are really browned, and not just gray.) Remove the steaks to a plate and set aside, and reduce the heat under the Dutch oven to medium-low.

2. Add the chopped onion, thyme, salt, and pepper and cook, stirring occasionally, until the onion is tender and translucent, about 15 minutes.

3. Meanwhile, in a separate skillet sauté the sliced onions in the remaining 1 tablespoon of olive oil over medium-low heat, stirring occasionally, until they are golden brown and very tender, about 45 minutes. Remove the sliced onions and set them aside.

4. To the chopped onions in the Dutch oven add the mushrooms, walnuts, and wine, increase the heat to high, and bring to a boil. Let the wine boil for 1 minute, reduce the heat to medium-low, and add the browned beef. Cover and simmer until the meat is very tender, about 90 minutes.

5. To serve, place a layer of sliced onions on each plate, top with a few pieces of cooked meat, and then spoon some of the mushroom-walnut mixture over the top. Serve warm.

Rousay, Orkney Islands, Scotland

DUMPLINGS *and* MINCE

Makes 8 dumplings, to serve 4

To me, this is truly the United Kingdom on a plate. Typically for British food, the dish uses dropped dumplings, not filled ones like pierogi or wontons. And the mince here is not the same thing that goes in a mince pie; it's just another word for ground beef. Put them together and you have the most British of poor man's foods. When I first find myself in rural Britain, I seek this dish out; and when I miss it, I make it at home.

> 1 tablespoon vegetable oil
> 1 cup chopped onion
> ½ cup chopped carrot
> 1 pound ground beef
> 2 cups all-purpose flour, plus more if needed
> 1 teaspoon baking powder
> ½ teaspoon dried sage
> ½ teaspoon dried thyme
> 1 teaspoon salt
> 1 teaspoon freshly ground black pepper
> ½ cup shredded beef suet or shortening
> 1½ cups water, plus more if needed
> 1 bay leaf
> Mashed or boiled potatoes, for serving

1. Heat the oil in a large skillet over medium heat. Add the onion and carrot and cook, stirring occasionally, until the onion starts to brown at the edges, about 15 minutes.

2. Add the ground beef and cook, stirring occasionally, until it is fully browned, about 30 minutes; if it's gray, it's not there yet. Use a wooden spoon to break up any clumps that form as the meat cooks.

3. While the beef is cooking, begin making the dumplings: Combine the flour, baking powder, sage, and thyme with ½ teaspoon of the salt and ½ teaspoon of the pepper in a large bowl and mix well.

4. Add the suet to the flour mixture and with your fingers, use a pinching motion to combine the ingredients. Add ½ cup of the water and work the mixture with your hands until a dough forms. If it's too dry, add a little more water, 1 tablespoon at a time, until the dough has the texture of modeling clay. If it's too soggy or sticky, add more flour, 1 tablespoon at a time, until the texture is correct. Divide the dough into 8 small balls and set aside.

5. Once the meat is browned, add the bay leaf, the remaining ½ teaspoon salt, ½ teaspoon pepper, and 1 cup water, and bring the liquid quickly to a simmer. Give the meat a few good stirs and put the 8 balls of dumpling dough on top. Reduce the heat to medium-low, cover the pot, and let it simmer until the dough has cooked through, about 20 minutes. If the tops of the dumplings are still raw looking, flip them over and cook for 10 minutes more. Serve warm, with mashed or boiled potatoes if you like.

CLASSIC ROAST BEEF *with* GRAVY

Makes 4 servings

What could be a better British meal than a Sunday lunch of roast beef at a friendly rural pub? With a few slices of beef, some well-made brown gravy on the plate, and some Yorkshire Pudding (page 159), this is as good as it gets. If it's not Sunday, or you're not in Britain, don't fret. The recipe is right here.

3 pounds boneless prime rib, rump, or top sirloin beef roast
1 teaspoon salt
1 teaspoon freshly ground black pepper
1 tablespoon dried rosemary
1 tablespoon dried thyme
2 tablespoons peanut oil or vegetable oil
2 tablespoons all-purpose flour
2 cups low-sodium beef broth
Yorkshire Pudding (optional; page 159), for serving

1. Preheat the oven to 300°F. Use a chef's knife to score the fat cap of the roast. You don't want to trim it off; just slice into it a bit, so that it renders easily and bastes the meat. Sprinkle the roast with the salt, pepper, rosemary, and thyme.

2. Heat the oil in a Dutch oven over medium-high heat and brown the roast over as much of its surface as possible, turning it every 3 or 4 minutes to keep things even. Remember, this step is called browning, not graying! Give it the 30 or so minutes it deserves, and you'll be rewarded with an extra shot of deliciousness.

3. Remove the Dutch oven from the heat, cover it with a tent of aluminum foil, and place in the preheated oven. (Don't use the pot lid, or you will end up with braised beef.) Roast for about 1 hour, until a meat thermometer inserted in the center of the roast reads 140°F. Transfer the beef to a serving plate, but keep the pan drippings in the pot.

4. Put the pot over medium heat on the stove top. Add the flour and cook, stirring frequently, until the flour is well browned, about 5 minutes.

5. Add the beef broth 2 tablespoons at a time, stirring continuously. Taste the gravy, which should be well seasoned from the pan drippings. If it's not, add additional salt and pepper to taste.

6. To serve, slice the roast beef, place on individual plates, and cover with the gravy. If you like, add a Yorkshire Pudding or two to each plate.

LANCASHIRE HOTPOT

Makes 4 servings

The technique of long, slow cooking is talked about these days as if it were a new invention. It's not new in Lancashire, where women have long assembled dishes like this one, dropped them off at local bakeries, and headed to work. Meanwhile, the bakers' ovens, cooling off from a night of bread making, would provide the gentle heat needed to perfectly cook this dish. On their way home, the women would grab their pots and feed their families.

   2 tablespoons unsalted butter, melted
   4 cups sliced potato
   4 shoulder lamb chops (about 1½ pounds total)
   2 teaspoons salt
   2 teaspoons freshly ground black pepper
   2 cups sliced onion
   2 cups low-sodium chicken broth

1. Preheat the oven to 225°F. Brush the bottom of a Dutch oven with some of the butter. Spread out half of the potatoes, and then place the lamb chops over them. Sprinkle the chops with some of the salt and pepper. Layer all of the onions on top of the chops, sprinkle with more salt and pepper, and cover with the remaining potatoes. Make sure the top layer of potatoes doesn't touch the cover of the pot.

2. Pour in the broth, brush the potatoes with the remaining butter, and sprinkle with the remaining salt and pepper. Cover the Dutch oven and bake for 8 hours. Check it every now and then to make sure nothing is burning. If the broth appears to be evaporating and the food is drying out, add water, ¼ cup at a time, until you once again have a broth.

3. Remove from the oven and let cool for 20 minutes. Serve warm.

VARIATION: If you use pork chops instead of lamb and replace the chicken broth with stout, you'll have an Irish hotpot.

CAWL: WELSH LAMB STEW

Makes 4 servings

Like chili and gumbo, cawl has its world champion (actually "champion of the world and elsewhere"—even bigger than chili), chosen each year in Saundersfoot, Wales. If a dish has its own championship, you know that it must be important. Indeed, cawl is often said to be the Welsh national dish, and it is worth seeking out.

1 pound lamb stew meat, cut into ½-inch cubes
2 cups coarsely chopped potato
2 cups coarsely chopped turnip
1 cup chopped parsnip
1 cup chopped carrot
1 teaspoon salt
½ teaspoon freshly ground black pepper
6 cups water
1¼ cups thinly sliced leek (about ¾ cup white part and
 ½ cup green part)
¼ cup chopped fresh flat-leaf parsley
Bread and butter, for serving
Cheddar cheese, for serving

1. Combine the lamb, potato, turnip, parsnip, carrot, salt, and pepper in a heavy soup pot and add the water. Bring to a simmer over medium heat and continue simmering the mixture, uncovered, stirring occasionally, until the lamb is tender, about 1½ hours. Skim the fat and foam from the liquid if necessary.

2. Add the leeks and parsley to the pot and simmer until the leeks are translucent, about 30 minutes more.

3. Serve the stew warm with bread, butter, and a piece of good cheddar cheese.

Taff River, Cardiff, Wales

pilgrimage: cawl

There's a game visitors to Wales play that I call Pronounce That Word. I'm not sure it's a fair game, though. The town of Porthmadog is pronounced *port-MAH-tic*, one of many examples that make it a tough game to win. And Wales's signature food, spelled *cawl*, is pronounced *cowl*, rhyming with *owl*. So if you go into a pub or restaurant in search of a bowl of *cawl* (see recipe, page 71) and you ask for *call*, people might not know what you're looking for. Call *cawl* something a bit different, like Welsh lamb stew, and you might be lucky enough to wind up with a bowl of stew and a language lesson—both very useful in Wales.

My first encounter with the Welsh language was on American television. I watched the Welsh pop singer Tom Jones pronounce the place name Llanfairpwllgwyngyllgogerychwyrndrobwllllantysiliogogogoch in one breath. The audience applauded wildly as if they'd all been trying themselves for hours and couldn't pull it off. I swore at that moment that if I ever went to Wales, Llanfairpwllgwyngyllgogerychwyrndrobwllllantysiliogogogoch would be my first stop. Sadly, though, in none of my first several dozen trips to Great Britain had I managed to go to Wales, and so I had never visited the town with the really long name.

One morning, in the English town of Shrewsbury, right on the Welsh border, I walked up to the train station ticket window and asked for "one to the Welsh place with the really long name." I had no idea how to pronounce it and didn't dare try. The ticket agent seemed thrilled to have the opportunity to cry out, "You mean Llanfairpwllgwyngyllgogerychwyrndrobwllllantysiliogogogoch, don't you?" The giant word just rolled off his tongue. He was obviously happy to show off his command of the Welsh language. I replied with a feeble "Yeah." I hoped for the best.

It turned out that Llanfairpwllgwyngyllgogerychwyrndrobwllllantysiliogogogoch was a "request stop"—the train stopped there only if a passenger asked—and the trainman made it clear that only those who could effortlessly pronounce the entire word could make the request. I was on the spot once again. Luckily, the crew pitied me and let me off.

The town consisted of a clothing and household goods store that had the look and feel of an L.L. Bean outlet, a few snack and souvenir shops, two pubs, a bridal salon, and a post office, much of it surrounding a large parking lot. I snapped a few photos of the Llanfairpwllgwyngyllgogerychwyrndrobwllllantysiliogogogoch train station and went into the tourist office. There a woman who obviously wasn't Welsh told me that she had never heard of cawl. Then, a second later, she asked me if it was

a food. I explained and she exclaimed, "Oh, the soup!"

Across from the parking lot I spotted the sort of café or lunchroom that looked like it should serve cawl—if only it were open. Then I tried a pub with a beautiful menu, but the guy behind the bar insisted he had never heard of the dish. That was followed by a conversation with a staff member of a second pub, who knew the dish and insisted it was out of season. Finally, I tried the snack bar of the huge Llanfairpwllgwyngyllgogerych-wyrndrobwllllantysiliogogogoch tourist center. There the reaction was different. Everybody knew what it was, but the answer was the same: They didn't have any. "How about a lovely piece of steak pie?" I was asked.

I hopped a bus to Bangor, a bigger town with a university. I started searching again, but without any luck. I settled for a ploughman's lunch (see sidebar, page 25) in a pub with free Wi-Fi.

I picked up the search again in Abergavenny, a hundred miles or so to the south. There, at a pub called the Hen and Chicks, at last I ate my first bowl of cawl in Wales. Washed down with a pint of Brain's, the local

bitter, it tasted like Irish stew made with lamb. I enjoyed the presentation, though: a bowl of stew on a larger plate with slices of bread, a bit of butter, and a piece of good cheese.

The next morning, I headed into the Welsh capital of Cardiff and started checking out menus. There cawl was so popular that I actually skipped places that didn't look appealing enough. In a small restaurant near the central market, I hit pay dirt, in the form of a flavorful stew with slivers of lamb in a thin sauce, which was more like a broth.

Not yet entirely satisfied, I went into the tourist office and asked, "Where's the best bowl of cawl in Cardiff?" They suggested a place that specialized in classic Welsh food called Y Mochyn Du ("The Black Pig"). I was a bit put off by the name, but I headed over there as soon as I was hungry enough to put down another bowl.

The place turned out to be filled with locals drinking the house ale and ordering from a menu that had both the Welsh classics and the sort of fancy menu writing that goes with the label *gastropub*. You know what I mean:

items like Soy-Glazed Roast Breast of Finchley Chicken or Ale-Braised Wolverhampton Dayboat Scallops. Like a good tourist, I ordered both a bowl of cawl and a plate of Welsh Rarebit (page 133) and settled down in front of the big-screen TV.

In Wales the big sport appears to be demolition derby played with people instead of cars. They call this rugby football. The whole bar was watching so intently that I managed to photograph my cawl and rarebit without attracting all that much atten-

tion. While the various teams of players demolished each other and racked up points, I tasted my cawl. It was a revelation, redolent with the flavor of parsnips, rutabaga, and leeks. More intense than gentle, a touch of wine would almost have made it French.

Boom! More rugby on the telly. Boom! More points on the scoreboard. Boom! The flavor of cawl exploded in my mouth. Okay, the Welsh rarebit was a bit too much like grilled cheese, but it was my first non-cawl dish in two days, so I didn't complain.

That night I tried to sleep, but craved another bowl of cawl. It was too late to find one. In the morning, I reminded myself that while a Welsh breakfast may have eggs, bacon, sausage, tomato, mushroom, cereal, fruit, fried bread, and toast, it doesn't include a bowl of lamb stew. And Llanfairpwllgwyngyllgogerychwyrndrobwllllantysiliogogogoch? Thinking it would attract tourists, it was given the name as a publicity stunt back in the 1860s. It worked.

CHICKEN *and* LEEK CASSEROLE

Makes 4 servings

Chicken and leeks seem to be an inspired combination, in Great Britain as elsewhere. Here we include them in a chicken casserole, a British cousin to an American chicken pie. You can also find the pair in a soup, Cock-a-leekie, on page 44.

¼ cup chopped British or Canadian bacon (see sidebar, page 91)
1 pound boneless, skinless chicken breast or thigh, cut into ½-inch pieces
2 cups chopped leek (white part only)
1 cup chopped carrot
1 teaspoon salt
½ teaspoon freshly ground black pepper
2 cups low-sodium chicken broth
1 cup beer or ale
¼ cup dried, unflavored bread crumbs

1. Preheat the oven to 325°F. Combine the bacon, chicken, leek, carrot, salt, pepper, broth, and beer in a Dutch oven or casserole and mix well so that the ingredients are evenly distributed.

2. Bake the casserole, covered, until the chicken is fully cooked, about 1 hour.

3. Remove the cover, return the casserole to the oven, and bake until about a third of the liquid has evaporated, about 30 minutes more.

4. Sprinkle the bread crumbs on top and return the casserole to the oven. Bake, uncovered, until the bread crumbs are nicely browned, about 30 minutes more. Serve warm.

LANCASHIRE HINDLE WAKES: CHICKEN *with* PRUNE *and* ALMOND STUFFING

Makes 4 servings

This was something served at wakes in a long-lost place called Hindle, in Lancashire. With prunes and almonds, the dish seems a bit medieval, and it is. It's also unique; I mean, how many boiled, stuffed whole chickens with a rich lemon sauce have you eaten lately?

1 cup chopped pitted prunes, plus 1 cup whole pitted prunes
½ cup fresh, unflavored bread crumbs
¼ cup chopped almonds
2 tablespoons shredded beef suet or shortening
3 tablespoons chopped fresh flat-leaf parsley
1 teaspoon chopped fresh sage
½ teaspoon dried marjoram
½ cup plus 1 tablespoon cider vinegar
1 teaspoon salt
½ teaspoon freshly ground black pepper
1 (3- to 4-pound) whole chicken
3 tablespoons brown sugar
2 tablespoons unsalted butter
2 tablespoons all-purpose flour
2 cups low-sodium chicken broth
2 large eggs, beaten
2 tablespoons fresh lemon juice
2 teaspoons grated lemon zest

1. Soak the chopped prunes in cold water for at least 1 hour and drain them. In a large bowl, combine the chopped prunes with the bread crumbs, almonds, suet, 1 tablespoon of the parsley, the sage and marjoram, 1 tablespoon of the vinegar, ½ teaspoon of the salt, and ¼ teaspoon of the pepper. Mix well, making sure all the ingredients are evenly distributed.

2. Rinse the chicken inside and out, pat it dry, and stuff it with the prune mixture. Use skewers or twine to close the chicken.

3. Combine the brown sugar and the remaining ½ cup of vinegar in a large pot with a tight-fitting lid. Put the stuffed chicken in the pot and add just enough water to cover the bird. Bring the liquid to a simmer over medium-low heat and cook the chicken, covered, until it is very tender and cooked all the way through, about 3 hours. Remove from the heat and leave the chicken in its cooking liquid, covered.

4. Melt the butter in a medium-size saucepan over medium-low heat. Mix in the flour with a wooden spoon and cook, stirring constantly, until the mixture is a thick paste. Continue cooking, stirring frequently, until the paste begins to brown, about 5 minutes more.

5. Add 2 tablespoons of the chicken stock to the flour and butter mixture and stir until the liquid is completely absorbed. Add the remaining chicken stock, 2 tablespoons at a time, stirring frequently, until you have a thick sauce in the pan. Remove from the heat.

6. Pour the beaten eggs in a large bowl. Add a tablespoon of the warm sauce, whisking constantly, to the beaten eggs. Repeat this step several times until the eggs are warmed but not scrambling. Then return the egg mixture to the sauce in the pan, whisking constantly. Stir in the lemon juice and zest and the remaining ½ teaspoon of salt and ¼ teaspoon of pepper, give the sauce a few more stirs, and set it aside.

7. Remove the cooked chicken from the cooking liquid and put it on a serving platter. Garnish with the whole prunes and the remaining 2 tablespoons of parsley. To serve, cut the chicken into pieces and then cover with the sauce. Although many people say this can be served cold or at room temperature, I find it's best served warm.

HOWTOWDIE: SCOTTISH ROAST CHICKEN

Makes 4 servings

In Scotland oats are everywhere, in oatcakes, oatmeal soup, and here, in a hearty stuffing for chicken.

2 tablespoons unsalted butter
5 medium-size onions, 1 chopped (about 1 cup) and
   4 quartered
1 cup rolled oats (not instant)
½ teaspoon dried sage
¼ teaspoon ground nutmeg
2 teaspoons salt
1½ teaspoons freshly ground black pepper
1 (2½- to 3½-pound) whole chicken
1 teaspoon dried rosemary

1. Preheat the oven to 375°F. Melt the butter in a saucepan over medium heat, add the chopped onion, and cook, stirring occasionally, until browned at the edges, about 15 minutes.

2. Mix in the oats, sage, nutmeg, 1 teaspoon of the salt, and ½ teaspoon of the pepper and cook the mixture until the oats begin to brown, about 5 minutes more. Remove from the heat and set aside.

3. Carefully wash the chicken inside and out, pat it dry, and stuff the cavity with the onion-oat mixture. Because the stuffing expands while it cooks, do not overfill the cavity. Close the cavity with one of those clips made for that purpose.

4. Put the chicken in a roasting pan and surround it with the onion quarters. Sprinkle with the remaining 1 teaspoon salt and 1 teaspoon pepper and the rosemary. Roast until a meat thermometer inserted between the thigh and breast reads 180°F, about 1½ hours. Let rest 10 minutes and serve.

DUNELM: SCOTTISH CHICKEN HASH

Makes 4 servings

With its chicken, button mushrooms, and cream sauce, served on toast wedges, dunelm might seem like something people ate back in the twenties, perhaps a Scottish answer to chicken à la king. It's a pleasant, comforting, and totally enjoyable dish.

1 tablespoon vegetable oil
1 teaspoon dried tarragon
1 pound boneless, skinless chicken breast or thigh, diced
2 cups sliced button mushrooms
1 teaspoon salt
½ teaspoon freshly ground black pepper
1 cup low-sodium chicken broth
1 tablespoon fresh lemon juice
3 tablespoons heavy cream
8 slices toast or Fried Bread (page 6), crusts cut off

1. Put the oil and tarragon in a skillet over medium heat and cook, stirring, until the herbs are well coated, about 1 minute.

2. Add the chicken, mushrooms, salt, and pepper and cook the mixture, stirring occasionally, until the chicken is cooked through and the mushrooms are tender, about 15 minutes.

3. Mix in the broth and lemon juice, increase the temperature to high, and bring the liquid to a boil. Let it boil for 1 minute, reduce the heat to medium-low, and simmer, uncovered, stirring occasionally, until half of the liquid evaporates, about 30 minutes.

4. Add the cream and continue simmering until the cream is well integrated into the sauce, about 3 minutes.

5. To serve, arrange the slices of toast on plates and ladle the chicken mixture over them. Serve warm.

FISH *and* CHIPS

Makes 4 servings

While some people now call Chicken Tikka Masala (page 110) Britain's national dish, it isn't the most famous or the only candidate. There's also fish and chips: deep-fried pieces of batter-dipped fish along with strips of lightly fried potato, often served with a side dish of the country's most misunderstood food, Mushy Peas (page 130).

So what's the difference between British chips and French fries? (Okay, *frites*.) Chips are cooked only once and therefore are a bit less crisp than their French cousins, the better for them to absorb condiments.

> 2 pounds flounder, pollock, or cod fillets, cut into 3 x 6-inch strips
> 1½ cups all-purpose flour
> ¼ cup cornstarch
> ½ teaspoon salt, plus more for the chips
> ½ teaspoon freshly ground black pepper, plus more for the chips
> 1 (12-ounce) bottle ale
> 3 quarts vegetable oil for frying
> 4 cups French fry–size potato strips

1. Use paper towels to pat the fish fillets dry. Whisk together the flour, cornstarch, salt, pepper, and ale in a large bowl until well combined—the mixture should have the look and texture of pancake batter. If it's too thick, add a little more ale; if it is too thin, add a bit more flour. Remember that a little bit of either goes a long way.

2. Pour the oil into a heavy 6- or 8-quart pot. You want at least 3 or 4 inches at the top of the pot so the hot oil does not overflow when the fish and potatoes are added.

3. Heat the oil until a deep-fry thermometer registers 375°F. Dip a piece of fish in the batter, and then use a slotted spoon to lower it into the hot oil. The oil is really going to foam up, so do not stand too close. Let the fish fry for 5 to 8 minutes, using the slotted spoon to turn the fillet in the oil if it cooks on only one side, until the crust is golden. Set aside to drain on paper towels and repeat with the remaining fillets.

4. Next cook the potatoes: Rinse the cut potato strips in water, and then pat them dry with a paper towel. Use a slotted spoon to lower a small batch of potatoes into the oil, which should still be at 375°F. As always, don't get your hands anywhere near the hot oil. Let the potatoes fry until golden, about 4 minutes. Remove with the slotted spoon and drain on paper towels. Repeat with small batches of the remaining potatoes. Season with salt and pepper.

5. Both the fish and the chips can be held in a warm oven for up to 40 minutes before serving. This is a much better choice than reheating them after they've cooled off. Often enough, fish and chips are eaten by themselves, but the most common sides are Mushy Peas (page 130) and curry sauce. True fish-and-chip purists insist that the proper drink to go alongside is hot tea. Diet soda marks you as a tourist.

frying tonight: some thoughts on fish and chips

Is a top-quality, stand-alone British fish-and-chip shop so much a thing of the past that we can't even imagine one anymore? Are we reduced to having our fish and chips in an establishment that also serves burgers and kabobs, or in a fancy sit-down place that does a range of seafood and is proud of its wine list?

Do we have to settle for one of the dismal-looking fish-and-chip shops that you find in almost every town of any size in the UK, with fluorescent lighting, steel counters, and big vats of brown frying oil? If Edward Hopper painted England, these shops would be his subject.

What you really want, and almost never see any longer, is a nice, clean place that fries locally caught fresh fish in the place's own made-on-the-premises batter, using clean oil. You'd think that you wouldn't need a fancy restaurant presided over by a celebrity chef to find fish and chips done this way—it's really just a basic and simple dish—but in Britain as elsewhere, nothing is harder to find than simple food cooked right.

I was reflecting on these matters after eating a dismal order of cod and chips in Newcastle one night. Sitting there and peeling the congealed mass of fish and potatoes apart, I tried to figure out what had gone wrong and realized the main problem was that the fish had been held—subjected to an additional stage of cooking when it was wrapped in paper and thereby steamed together with the potatoes.

What, then, does a person look for in a chip shop? More than anything, there should be no fried items on display when you walk in. If they take their fish or their chips prefried from a display case or, even worse, a large bin, turn your back and walk away. Long lines aren't much of a clue; they could mean low prices, or special deals, or perhaps a great review from a local critic who knows no better. If the place has tables and waiter service, the odds are on your side; it probably has a regular clientele that comes back because the food is fried to order.

There's a secret of sorts I'd like to share: Reliable, inexpensive fish and chips can be had at fishermen's missions. These are a sort of hostel for the crews of fishing boats, and they are located in most serious ports. From Newlyn in Cornwall, England, to Scrabster in Scotland, you'll find quality fish for an audience that wouldn't have it any other way.

If you're not going to be in a town with a fishermen's mission, you might find my accompanying chart useful. It might not lead to the sublime, but it will keep you out of trouble.

choose a chip shop

clue	points	reason
Boasts "Best in Britain"	–2	Unlikely to be true
Boasts "Our fish are skinless and boneless."	+1	Reasonable claim, probably correct
Burgers and kabobs on menu	–1	Not focused enough
Calls a complete meal a "fish tea"	+2	A traditional description that appeals to locals
Fried pizza or fried candy bars on menu	+1	This place takes frying seriously
Fish other than cod or haddock	+2	Could be making an effort to use fresh and local products; ask.
Has a wine list	–2	The only proper drink is tea
Honestly tells you it uses frozen fish	+2	Better than four-day-old "fresh"
Nothing but fish, chips, peas, and tea on the menu	+3	Fish-frying purist, likely to pursue quality as a goal
Pre-fried fish behind glass	–3	Deal breaker; food must be fried to order
Uses pre-battered fish	–2	Can be bought in the supermarket for half the price

Note: There is no official scoring system.
The more points the better.

FISH CAKES

Makes 8 cakes, to serve 4

Don't have access to, or a budget for, the fanciest fillets? Are you cooking fish for people who are not the biggest fish fans? These fish cakes offer a solution. With any inexpensive white, flaky fish and just a few other ingredients, you can serve satisfying and tasty fish without breaking the bank. Do you want your kids to eat more fish? Call them fish burgers, serve them in buns, and you're all set.

1½ pounds flaky white fish fillets, such as whiting,
    flounder, haddock, or tilapia
4 fresh or canned anchovy fillets
1 teaspoon hot mustard
2 large eggs
2 tablespoons chopped fresh dill
3 tablespoons chopped fresh flat-leaf parsley
1 teaspoon freshly ground white pepper
3 cups cooked potatoes
1 teaspoon salt
Tartar sauce, Worcestershire sauce, or Liquor (page 143),
    for serving

1. Preheat the oven to 325°F. Combine the fish fillets, anchovies, mustard, and eggs in a food processor and pulse until all the ingredients are broken up and well blended.

2. Combine the fish mixture, dill, parsley, pepper, cooked potato, and salt in a large bowl and mix with your hands or a large spoon until well blended.

3. Oil a baking sheet. Form the fish-potato mixture into 8 patties. Bake the fish cakes until the tops have just begun to brown, about 30 minutes. Turn them over and bake them until the other side has browned, about 20 minutes more. Serve warm with tartar sauce, Worcestershire sauce, or Liquor.

Tenby, Wales

FRIED SMELTS

Makes 4 servings

These days when people go to their local fishmonger, they tend to start with the most expensive items and work their way down. Some people will give up if the tuna, swordfish, and wild-caught salmon aren't up to snuff. I'd like to suggest a different strategy: Start at the bottom. There you'll find smelts, that old British classic. These tiny fish are inexpensive and loaded with flavor.

> 4 tablespoons (½ stick) unsalted butter
> 2 pounds cleaned and gutted smelts
> ¼ cup capers, rinsed and drained
> ¼ cup chopped fresh flat-leaf parsley
> 1 teaspoon salt (optional)
> 1 teaspoon freshly ground black pepper (optional)

1. Melt the butter in a skillet over medium heat, taking care not to let the butter burn. Add the smelts and stir gently, making sure they are not breaking apart. Cook, stirring occasionally, until they are well coated with butter and just about cooked through, about 10 minutes.

2. Mix in the capers and parsley and continue cooking, stirring occasionally, until the smelts begin to brown, about 5 minutes more. Taste a smelt, and, if it needs it, add the salt and pepper. Give the smelts a few more stirs and remove them from the heat. Serve warm.

Roast Pork *with* Apricot *and* Walnut Stuffing

Makes 6 servings

The raisins, apricots, and walnuts in this dish give the pork rich, sweet accents as well as an interesting texture. Serve it with some roast potatoes on a cold, damp night, and feel its warmth.

4 tablespoons (½ stick) unsalted butter
1 cup chopped onion
½ cup raisins
¼ cup chopped fresh flat-leaf parsley
1 cup dried, unflavored bread crumbs
1 cup diced dried apricots
1 cup chopped walnuts
1 (2½-pound) boneless pork shoulder roast
1 teaspoon salt
1 teaspoon freshly ground black pepper

1. Preheat the oven to 325°F. Melt the butter in a skillet over medium heat and add the onion. Cook, stirring occasionally, until the onion is translucent and browning at the edges, about 15 minutes.

2. Stir in the raisins, parsley, bread crumbs, apricots, and walnuts. Remove from the heat and set aside.

3. Untie the roast and lay it out on a work surface. Use a meat mallet to flatten out the meat a bit. Spread as much of the onion and apricot stuffing as you can over the surface of the meat and sprinkle it with the salt and pepper; reserve the remaining stuffing. Roll the roast back up and tie it tightly with twine at 3-inch intervals.

4. Oil a roasting pan, and spread out the remaining stuffing on the bottom. Place the stuffed roast in the pan, cover with a tent of aluminum foil, and roast for about 2 hours, or until a meat thermometer inserted in the center reads 165°F. Check the roast every 30 minutes or so while it's cooking, and if the bed of stuffing on the bottom of the pan starts to dry out, add a cup of water.

5. Remove the roast from the oven and let it rest for 10 minutes. Slice and serve warm.

is that bacon? british versus american bacon

The first time I visited an English snack truck, I saw that it offered "bacon sandwiches." I myself had nothing but tea that time, but I noticed that the bacon sandwich was one of the truck's most popular items.

I assumed the worst: half a dozen bacon strips, the same stuff that some Americans put next to eggs or on top of a burgers, slapped between slices of white bread. Eventually I learned I was wrong, and regretted avoiding bacon sandwiches for so many years.

I simply needed to grasp the British definition of "bacon."

For us, it's the cured, and often smoked, belly of pork. For them, other parts of the pig are called "bacon," too, just as long as they're cured and sliced.

Two kinds of bacon are sold in the UK. What the Brits call "streaky" bacon is just like the American stuff. What they simply call "bacon" is typically a boneless pork chop that's cured, sliced thin, and fried. While I wouldn't exactly call a British bacon sandwich "lean," it's much more than just slices of fat between slices of bread.

Ffest y Cybydd: Miser's Feast

Makes 4 servings

Isn't a miser someone who deprives himself of the good things in life? Things that may include a feast once in a while, for example? While the word *miser* might have such negative connotations, frugality is a trait that the British have long admired. That's where this traditional Welsh dish comes in. Simply put, it's a big plate of potatoes and pork—cheap and delicious food.

Originally, recipes for a miser's feast called for British bacon, and the addition of pork chops was considered a luxury. But these days the situation has reversed. High-quality British bacon is a bit of a luxury, and pork chops are the poor man's meat. You can make it either way. British bacon (see sidebar, page 91) will give you a historically authentic dish. It harks back to the days before refrigeration, when cured pork products like bacon were a staple.

3 cups sliced potato
2 cups sliced onion
1 pound pork chops, thinly sliced
3 cups water
1 teaspoon salt
½ teaspoon freshly ground black pepper

1. Preheat the oven to 325°F. Oil a 9 x 13-inch baking dish or a Dutch oven. In layers, place the potato, onion, and pork in the dish or pot. Pour in the water, and sprinkle with the salt and pepper.

2. Bake, covered (use foil for a baking dish), for 1 hour, or until the pork is cooked through and the potatoes are very tender. Uncover and bake for 30 minutes more, or until the liquid thickens into a sauce. Serve warm, as a one-dish meal.

Faggots

Makes 16 meatballs, to serve 4

There are certain people in Great Britain who will see the word *faggot* on a pub menu and simply forget that anything else is available. It's that powerfully tempting to some, and just as powerfully repulsive to others. For us speakers of American English, the name of the dish is one of the most baffling we have ever encountered. Yes, there's some relief when a plate of what looks like meatballs in brown gravy is set in front of you, but their taste is much more intense and unusual than what we normally find on top of spaghetti. The traditional way to serve faggots is alongside mashed potatoes or chips (page 83) and gravy.

> 4 ounces American ("streaky") bacon
> 8 ounces beef liver or calf liver
> 1 cup chopped onion
> 1 cup dried, unflavored bread crumbs
> 1 pound ground pork
> ¼ cup chopped fresh flat-leaf parsley
> 1 tablespoon dried sage
> 1 teaspoon salt
> ½ teaspoon freshly ground black pepper
> Mashed potatoes and gravy (optional), for serving

1. Preheat the oven to 325°F. Combine the bacon, liver, and onion in a food processor and pulse until you have a coarse paste. Transfer to a large mixing bowl.

2. Add the bread crumbs, pork, parsley, sage, salt, and pepper and mix well—your hands are great for this—until all the ingredients are well combined. Form the meat into balls about 2 inches in diameter and place them on a well-oiled cookie sheet.

3. Bake for about 45 minutes, or until the outsides are browned. Cut one open to make sure the faggots are cooked all the way through. Serve with mashed potatoes and gravy if you like.

LAMB'S TONGUE *with* RAISIN SAUCE

Makes 4 servings

Have you seen a sauce like this before? When I first encountered it in Britain, it reminded me of the sauces for ham that turn up in the American South. Lamb's tongue is as British as it gets, though. Substitute a veal tongue, if you wish, or if your butcher says that is easier to get. Whether you are using lamb or veal tongue, don't forget to peel it right after it comes out of the pot.

3 pounds lamb's tongue (about 6 to 8 tongues)
1 cup chopped carrot
1 cup chopped celery
1 cup chopped onion
1 sprig fresh flat-leaf parsley
1 tablespoon plus ¼ teaspoon salt
3 quarts water
½ cup packed light brown sugar
1 tablespoon cornstarch
½ teaspoon powdered mustard
1 cup low-sodium chicken broth
3 tablespoons malt vinegar
½ cup raisins
1 lemon, peel on, sliced crosswise

1. Put the tongue, carrot, celery, onion, parsley, and 1 tablespoon of the salt in a large soup pot and pour in the water. Bring to a boil over high heat and continue boiling for 1 minute. Reduce the heat to medium-low and simmer, covered, for 45 minutes, or until the tongue is tender. Set aside.

2. Meanwhile, make the sauce: Put the remaining ¼ teaspoon salt and the brown sugar, cornstarch, and mustard in a saucepan. Over low heat, add the broth and vinegar, a little at a time, stirring constantly, until all the liquid has been added and the dry ingredients have dissolved.

3. Add the raisins and lemon slices to the sauce mixture, increase the heat to medium, and bring the sauce to a simmer. Cook, stirring occasionally, until the raisins are plump and the sauce has thickened, about 15 minutes.

4. To assemble the dish for serving, remove the tongue from the cooking liquid, cut it into thin slices, and arrange the slices on a plate. (You can discard the cooking vegetables.) Spoon the sauce over the meat and serve warm.

Rag Pudding

Makes 4 servings

There comes a point when you have enough experience with British food to know that the name of a dish doesn't necessarily tell you what's inside. So when I first saw rag pudding on a café menu a few years ago, I didn't think for even a second that I would be eating rags. The *rag* refers to the cheesecloth in which the dish is cooked. Will it wind up on your plate? It doesn't have to, but it could.

3 cups all-purpose flour, plus more if needed
2 teaspoons baking powder
½ cup shredded beef suet or shortening
6 quarts plus 1 cup water, plus more if needed
1 pound beef chuck steak, diced
8 ounces lamb kidneys, cleaned, deveined, and diced
1 cup chopped onion
1 teaspoon salt
½ teaspoon freshly ground black pepper

1. Combine the flour, baking powder, and suet in a large bowl. Use a pinching motion with your fingers to combine them into something that feels like bread crumbs.

2. Add 1 cup of the water to the flour and stir together with a wooden spoon to form a dough. If it's too dry, add more water, 1 tablespoon at a time, until you have the right texture. If it's too soft or soggy, add flour, again, 1 tablespoon at a time, until you have a dough.

3. Turn the dough out onto a floured work surface and roll it out into an 8 x 16-inch rectangle about ¼ inch thick. Fold the cheesecloth into an 18 x 24-inch rectangle with 4 or 5 layers of thickness. Lay it out on a flat surface, and put the dough on it.

4. Put the steak, kidneys, and onion on half the dough, leaving a border so it can be sealed, and sprinkle with the salt and pepper. Then fold the dough over the filling to form a package. Pinch the seams to seal it shut so that no water can enter. Wrap the cheesecloth around the package (rolling works best for me), pull it tight, and secure it with safety pins. No dough should be exposed; it should all be covered with cheesecloth.

5. Pour 6 quarts of water into a large soup pot and put in the wrapped pudding. Bring the water to a boil over high heat and let it boil for 1 minute. Reduce the heat to medium-low and let the pudding simmer, covered, until the meats are completely cooked and tender, about 2 hours.

6. Use tongs or a very large slotted spoon to remove the pudding from the pot. Drain in a colander, and let it cool for about 10 minutes. To serve, transfer to a platter and unwrap the warm pudding at the table.

TRIPE *and* ONIONS

Makes 4 servings

For too many people, tripe is a test of sorts. Eat it, and you're somehow "authentic." Cook it well, and you're more than someone who just throws burgers on the grill. It shouldn't be this way. Tripe is inexpensive, and when cooked properly, it's delicious. Not long ago, British towns of any size had a tripe shop—or at least a tripe vendor with a stall at the local market. Tripe was sold either cooked or ready to throw into the pot, and tripe sandwiches were a favorite. These days tripe is making a comeback as an ingredient favored by such British luminaries as Gordon Ramsay, Fergus Henderson, and Rick Stein. Perhaps those little shops will come back.

The 3 pounds of tripe may seem like a huge amount, but it will shrink considerably as it is cooked.

- 4 quarts water
- 3 pounds honeycomb tripe, cut into 1-inch pieces
- 1 tablespoon plus ½ teaspoon salt
- 4 cups whole milk
- 1 bay leaf
- ¼ teaspoon ground nutmeg
- 2 cups sliced onion
- 2 tablespoons unsalted butter
- 2 tablespoons all-purpose flour
- 2 tablespoons chopped fresh flat-leaf parsley

1. Bring the water to a boil over high heat in a large pot. Add the tripe and 1 tablespoon of the salt. Let the tripe boil for 3 minutes, reduce the heat to medium-low, and let it simmer, covered, until it starts to become tender, about 1 hour. Remove from the heat, drain off the water, and return the tripe to the pot.

2. Add the remaining ½ teaspoon salt, the milk, bay leaf, nutmeg, and onion. Simmer, uncovered, over medium-low heat, stirring occasionally, until the liquid has reduced by a third and the tripe is tender, about 1 hour. Remove the tripe and reserve the remaining liquid.

3. Melt the butter in a skillet over medium heat, whisk in the flour, and cook, stirring frequently, until there are no lumps and the flour begins to brown, about 5 minutes. Add the reserved cooking liquid to the butter and flour mixture, a few tablespoons at a time, stirring constantly. You will soon have a thick sauce.

4. Stir in the cooked tripe and bring the liquid to a boil. The sauce will thicken even more within a minute or two. When that happens, remove it from the heat and sprinkle with the parsley. Serve warm.

The
CURRY SHOP

I f there's one thing that everybody in Great Britain eats, it's curry. Some will choose a searingly hot phal or vindaloo, others a relatively mild dish like a korma. In this curry-crazed country, you can find it in any form, from frozen, canned, and a host of other instant preparations in the supermarket to elegant presentations at four-star restaurants. The best curry of all for me, though, is made from scratch in my own kitchen.

where did curry come from?

Here's the mystery. Scattered around the British Isles are thousands of shops and restaurants, all apparently unrelated, serving dishes that are not found anywhere else on the planet. They're staffed by people of similar ethnic backgrounds, and your first thought would be that the food they're serving comes from their homelands. But did they really eat mushroom *bhaji* in their home country?

In Britain, people will swear up and down that this is real Indian food. Corner take-away shops will boast of the authenticity of their offerings, but South Asians who haven't spent time in the UK aren't likely to recognize a single dish they serve.

The most common explanation is that the foods Britons call *curry* were first cooked by Bangladeshi fishermen looking for a way to re-create the flavors of home in a cramped ship's galley. Over the years, they produced a small handful of pastes and concentrates that could be made in advance, easily stored, and recombined into a wide variety of dishes. When some of these fishermen immigrated to England, they found that selling those bases, and the food made with them, was a good business.

In short, curry in Britain is an expression of the melting pot of the British Empire. I am constantly asked when curry became British, and my answer is, "At least fifty years ago." Britons have been making South Asian–inspired dishes for far longer, but that's when the full embrace began.

CHICKEN KORMA

Makes 4 servings

With a mild and creamy yogurt-based sauce, chicken korma is curry house comfort food, and it's easy to make at home.

- 2 tablespoons unsalted butter or ghee (clarified butter)
- 3 bay leaves
- 2 teaspoons ground coriander
- 1 teaspoon chili powder
- ½ teaspoon ground cinnamon
- ½ teaspoon ground cardamom
- 4 whole cloves
- 2 teaspoons ground cumin
- 2 cups chopped onion
- 2 tablespoons grated fresh ginger
- 6 garlic cloves, crushed and finely chopped
- 1 cup canned crushed tomatoes
- 1 pound boneless, skinless chicken breast, cut into 1-inch pieces
- ½ teaspoon salt
- 1 cup water
- ½ cup plain yogurt
- ½ cup fresh or frozen shredded unsweetened coconut
- 2 tablespoons chopped fresh cilantro
- Basmati rice (optional), for serving

1. Melt the butter in a skillet or wok over high heat and add the bay leaves, coriander, chili powder, cinnamon, cardamom, cloves, and cumin. Cook, stirring constantly, until the spices just begin to smoke, about 3 minutes.

2. Reduce the heat to medium and mix in the onion, ginger, and garlic. Cook, stirring occasionally, until the onion is limp and translucent, about 30 minutes.

3. Add the tomato, chicken, salt, and water. Bring to a simmer and continue simmering, uncovered, stirring occasionally, until the chicken is cooked through and about a third of the liquid has evaporated, about 40 minutes.

4. Mix in the yogurt and coconut and cook, stirring constantly, until the yogurt is completely incorporated into the dish, about 3 minutes. Remove the bay leaves and stir in the chopped cilantro. Remove from the heat and serve warm, preferably with rice on the side.

VARIATION: You can make this dish a vegetarian one by substituting 4 cups of cubed eggplant for the chicken. Why the larger quantity? The eggplant will shrink more as it cooks.

pilgrimage: lost in the balti triangle

Balti is the name of a dish you'll see all over the United Kingdom, and these days, in Indian restaurants around the world. It is a sort of stir-fried curry with lamb, beef, shrimp, or vegetables. But where does it come from?

First of all, there's a place called Baltistan. It's a region in Pakistan that borders China, not far from Tibet. And there's a thing called a *balti,* too—a woklike pot used by Balti cooks.

But the real home of the curry dishes called Balti isn't any place in Pakistan. Instead, it's in the Sparkbrook and Sparkhill sections of the English city of Birmingham, in an area collectively known as the Balti Triangle. Home to immigrants from the Balti region who cook in baltis, it's only fair that the cuisine they've created has become known as Balti.

Today Ladypool Road, the main drag of Sparkbrook, combines sights and sensations that are surprisingly familiar to Americans. Here South Asian teenagers drive up and down the street blasting American rap music while shoppers crowd sari and food stores. On a sunny day, it's like being in the Bronx. Only it's a British sort of Bronx, with really narrow streets and one restaurant after another. When a boy in pajamas begged me for a cigarette in pidgin English, I knew I had left the Cotswolds behind.

I started my first day in Birmingham at Popular Balti, a takeout shop on Ladypool Road. Here the menu claimed to offer "authentic Kasmiri Balti dishes" and was filled with items that have never appeared on a menu outside Birmingham. I ordered Balti *keema* and spinach along with mushroom *bhaji* and a tandoori naan bread. My plate combined flavors you expect in an Indian restaurant with the distinct taste and texture of stir-frying. In many places I had been in Great Britain, Balti was just another curry, but here it was

a different thing entirely. The menu listed dozens of combinations, some just a couple of ingredients thrown into the wok (Oops! I mean the *balti*!), others more complex. Some were Balti variations of classic British curries, like Balti meat korma or Balti chicken *dhansak*.

Meanwhile, two guys came in, sat down, and told the waiter, "We just want sausage and chips; we can't eat this weird stuff." The waiter started laughing and talking soccer. It was obvious that these guys were kidding, and in fact regulars. It turned out they were both restaurant professionals who often drive a forty-mile round-trip to eat at the Popular. "This is the place that defines it for the others," one said as they passed down pieces of tandoori meat to me. I couldn't thank them, or the chef, enough.

On a bank holiday Monday a few days later, street vendors started spilling their way onto Stratford Road, another of the Balti Triangle's major shopping streets.

But instead of Balti dishes, authentic street foods from Pakistan were being offered. There were the bright orange sweets called *jelebi*, as well as samosas, pakoras, and all sorts of meat kebabs.

I started with a meat samosa and some vegetable pakoras and then went on to a lamb dish called a *paratha kebab*. All were assertively spiced and delicious. A few blocks later, I sat down at a restaurant that appeared to cater to people from the neighborhood. They had Bollywood music videos blasting, lines out the door, and no Baltis at all on the menu. I had shish kebabs with salad and a large naan bread. It was really simple food, perfectly cooked, and the price was less than a burger and fries at home. The quality beat any South Asian restaurant in the States.

It was maddening. Every time a restaurant staff member told me about relatives in America, I wanted to cry out, "Why don't they open a restaurant with food this good?" I always stopped myself by

recalling that lamb is a hard sell at home, and intensely salted and spiced dishes aren't any easier. Everything I ate was a kaleidoscope of different seasonings, combined with strongly flavored meat—a food fanatic's dream.

On another outing into the Balti Triangle, I stopped in at a restaurant called King's Paradise, where the placemats read, "From mild to hot, we've got the lot." Because it was my last night in Birmingham, I blew the bank and ordered the "special Balti," from what I now understood to be a classic Balti restau-

rant menu, as well as a tandoori naan and some salad. The King's Paradise was every bit as good as the Popular but the food had stronger fresh herbal flavors.

The meals I enjoyed in the Balti Triangle weren't the sort of elegant fare one is often offered in South Asian restaurants in London, or even a few miles away in downtown Birmingham. There was soul in these simple dishes, a persuasiveness that a cook needs when he's trying to take what he knows and make it work in a very foreign environment. And work it does.

ONE-POT BALTI
Makes 4 servings

Many Balti recipes call for an oily paste of spices that have to be prepared separately, but here we use a quick-cooking stir-fried method and make the dish in one pot. So get ready and have your ingredients measured first and your wok, or a large skillet, on the stove. By curry standards, the action proceeds rapidly. Garlic-ginger paste is available in Indian markets.

1 teaspoon chili powder
½ teaspoon garam masala powder
½ teaspoon ground turmeric
½ teaspoon ground cumin
1 teaspoon ground coriander
½ teaspoon salt
2 tablespoons unsalted butter or ghee (clarified butter)
2 teaspoons tamarind concentrate
2 tablespoons garlic-ginger paste
2 cups sliced onion
1 cup carrot strips
1 cup chopped tomato
2 cups red or yellow bell pepper strips
2 cups cauliflower florets
¼ cup water, plus more as needed (optional)
2 tablespoons chopped fresh cilantro
Basmati rice, for serving
Naan (optional), for serving

1. Mix the chili powder, garam masala, turmeric, cumin, coriander, and salt together in a small bowl.

2. Combine the butter, tamarind, garlic-ginger paste, and dry spices in a large skillet or wok over high heat. Cook, stirring, until the dry spices are coated with butter, about 1 minute.

3. Add the onions and carrots and cook, stirring very frequently, until the onions are limp and begin to brown, about 5 minutes.

4. Add the tomatoes, bell peppers, and cauliflower and cook, stirring frequently, until the cauliflower is tender, about 8 minutes more. If the ingredients start to dry out, add water, ¼ cup at a time, until a thick sauce forms.

5. Toss in the cilantro, give the mixture a few stirs, and remove from the heat. Serve right away, with the basmati rice and, if you like, naan.

VARIATIONS: Replace the cauliflower with 1 pound of beef, lamb, or chicken, cut into small strips. A pound of peeled raw shrimp is great, too. Or, for a more substantial vegetarian version, keep the cauliflower and add 2 cups of diced tofu or *paneer*.

LAMB DOPIAZA

Makes 4 servings

Stewed meat with savory gravy: What could be a more perfect pub meal? Here the savory flavor comes from onions; *dopiaza* is an Urdu word that means "having two kinds of onions" or "double onions." It makes for a great British curry. Don't be put off by the large quantity of onions—they're what give the dish its earthiness.

¼ cup peanut oil
4 cups sliced onion, plus 2 cups chopped onion
   (about 4 large onions total)
½ teaspoon ground cinnamon
3 bay leaves
5 whole cardamom pods
5 whole cloves
1 teaspoon salt
1 pound boneless lamb stew meat, cut into ½-inch cubes
6 garlic cloves, crushed and chopped
1 tablespoon shredded fresh ginger
1 teaspoon ground cumin
1 teaspoon ground coriander
1 cup plain whole-milk yogurt
1 teaspoon garam masala powder
1 teaspoon chili powder
1 cup water
Basmati rice, for serving
Chutney, for serving (for example, Fruit Chutney,
   page 195)

1. Combine the oil and the sliced onions in a large soup pot over medium-low heat and cook, stirring occasionally, until the onions are caramelized, about 45 minutes. Remove the onions from the oil and set them aside, leaving the onion-flavored oil in the pot.

2. In the same pot sauté the cinnamon, bay leaves, cardamom pods, cloves, and salt briefly over high heat until the spices are coated with oil, about 30 seconds.

3. Reduce the heat to medium and add the lamb. Cook, stirring, until the lamb is well browned, about 15 minutes. Take the meat out of the pot and set it aside.

4. Add the garlic, ginger, cumin, coriander, and chopped onions and cook, stirring occasionally, until the onions turn translucent and begin to brown at the edges, about 15 minutes.

5. Stir in the yogurt, garam masala, chili powder, and water, and then add the browned meat. Reduce the heat to medium-low and simmer, covered, until the meat is tender, about 1 hour. Uncover and continue to simmer, stirring occasionally, until about a third of the liquid has evaporated and you have a thick sauce, about 30 minutes more.

6. Add the reserved sliced onions to the cooked meat, stir a few times, and simmer, uncovered, until the onions are heated through, about 3 minutes. Remove the bay leaves and serve warm with basmati rice and chutney.

CHICKEN TIKKA MASALA

Makes 4 servings

You find chicken tikka masala everywhere in Great Britain, so much so that it almost seems like the country's national dish. Of course it's in curry shops and small-town Indian restaurants. It's on the curry menus you find in pubs, too. This dish is so pervasive that you'll even see it as a filling in sandwich shops. If that doesn't appeal to you, cut the chicken into small pieces and serve it as a party snack, or as a topping for a large green salad. But the traditional way to serve this dish is plated with basmati rice.

In practice, this is two recipes: chicken tikka and Masala Sauce, which goes over it. Legend has it that chicken tikka has been around for a long time, but the idea of serving it with Masala Sauce is a more recent modification. Masala Sauce also can be served over the recipe that follows it, Tofu Tikka (page 113), or even over plain chicken, burgers, or fish.

1 cup yogurt
2 tablespoons chopped fresh ginger
2 tablespoons crushed and chopped garlic cloves
1 tablespoon ground cumin
1 tablespoon garam masala powder (preferable) or curry powder
1 teaspoon crushed red chile flakes
½ teaspoon saffron
2 boneless, skinless chicken breasts (about 1 pound total)
1 recipe Masala Sauce (recipe follows)

1. Stir together the yogurt, ginger, garlic, cumin, garam masala, chile flakes, and saffron in a medium-size nonreactive bowl until the mixture is well combined.

2. Cut the chicken breasts into strips 1 inch wide and put them in the yogurt and spice mixture. Toss to make sure the chicken is well coated. Place in the refrigerator for at least 3 hours, or up to 1 day.

3. Preheat the oven to 325°F. Oil a baking sheet and spread out the chicken pieces on it. Bake for 30 minutes, or until the chicken is cooked through and the surface is dry. Serve right away with Masala Sauce.

MASALA SAUCE

Makes 2 cups

2 tablespoons unsalted butter or ghee (clarified butter)
1 teaspoon ground cumin
1 teaspoon ground coriander
½ teaspoon ground turmeric
½ teaspoon crushed red chile flakes
1 tablespoon chopped fresh ginger
6 garlic cloves, crushed and chopped
2 cups chopped onion
1 cup canned crushed tomatoes
1 teaspoon sugar
½ teaspoon salt
1 cup whole milk
Chopped fresh cilantro for garnish

1. Melt the butter in a saucepan over medium heat and add the cumin, coriander, turmeric, chile flakes, ginger, and garlic and sauté, stirring occasionally, until the garlic begins to brown at the edges, about 12 minutes.

2. Reduce the heat to low and add the onion. Cook, stirring occasionally, until the onion turns golden, about 40 minutes. Do not hurry this step: You'll wind up burning the garlic and you won't release the natural sugars in the onion. This extra time is the key to success.

3. Add the tomatoes and cook, stirring occasionally, for 10 minutes more, until the raw taste is gone. Mix in the sugar, salt, and milk and continue cooking, stirring occasionally, until much of the liquid has evaporated and you have a thick sauce in the pan, about 30 minutes. Garnish with the cilantro.

Tofu Tikka Masala

Makes 4 servings

What's the vegetarian choice today? It's a common enough question. In Britain, where non–meat eaters seem to be everywhere, the person ordering up the vegetarian special may be right next to the guy who's enjoying his blood sausage and roast beef—there's always a selection. For tikka, tofu is the best choice. It bakes up well and holds the tikka marinade and Masala Sauce nicely.

> 4 cakes or 1 (14-ounce) package firm tofu
> 2 cups yogurt
> ¼ cup chopped fresh ginger
> ¼ cup crushed and chopped garlic cloves (from about 10 cloves)
> 2 tablespoons ground cumin
> 2 tablespoons curry powder
> 2 teaspoons crushed red chile flakes
> 1 teaspoon saffron
> 1 recipe Masala Sauce (page 111)
> Basmati rice, for serving

1. Rinse and drain the tofu cakes, cut them into 1-inch cubes, and pat them dry. Set them aside to dry a bit more.

2. Combine the yogurt, ginger, garlic, cumin, curry powder, chile flakes, and saffron in a large nonreactive bowl. Add the tofu pieces and toss gently until they are coated with the yogurt mixture. Cover the bowl and let the mixture marinate in the refrigerator for at least 6 hours, or up to 2 days.

3. Preheat the oven to 325°F. Oil a baking sheet and place the tofu pieces on it, leaving plenty of space between them. Bake for 1 hour, or until the surface of the tofu appears dry and crisp. Turn the tofu cakes over 3 or 4 times during baking so they cook evenly. Serve with Masala Sauce and basmati rice.

ONION BHAJI

Makes 4 servings

Onion *bhaji* is the fried appetizer that has begun more than a few million British curry meals. It's a typical fritter made from that most common of Indian ingredients, the onion. And its chickpea flour batter reminds us of its origins too. When it's all put together and deep-fried, something great appears. Give it a try.

1 cup chickpea flour
1 cup all-purpose flour
1 teaspoon baking powder
1 teaspoon ground cumin
½ teaspoon cayenne pepper
½ teaspoon ground coriander
1 teaspoon salt
½ teaspoon freshly ground white pepper
1 large egg
1 cup water, plus more as needed
2 cups sliced onion
Oil for deep-frying
Chutney (for example, Fruit Chutney, page 195; optional), for serving

1. Combine the chickpea flour, all-purpose flour, baking powder, cumin, cayenne, coriander, salt, and pepper in a large bowl and mix well.

2. Whisk in the egg and water. You should have a batter, not a dough. If it's too thick to coat the onions, add more water, ¼ cup at a time. If the batter is too thin and just runs off anything dipped in it, add all-purpose flour, again ¼ cup at a time, until it is nice and thick. Toss the onion slices in the batter until every piece is well coated.

3. Prepare to deep-fry the onions: Have ready a heavy pot, a deep-fry thermometer, a slotted spoon, and a place to drain the *bhaji* as they come out of the pot. Pour the oil into the pot to a depth of at least 4 inches; the pot should not be more than two-thirds full, though. Heat the oil to 375°F on your thermometer.

4. Take about ¼ cup of the onion and batter mixture and add it to the hot oil. Let it deep-fry until golden brown, about 2 minutes. Use a slotted spoon to remove from the oil, and set aside to drain on paper towels. Repeat with the rest of the battered onions. You can fry more than one fritter at a time, but don't crowd the pot. Serve warm, with chutney if you like.

Onion Relish

Makes 2 cups relish, to serve 8

You might not see this very often in the States, but have you ever been seated in a British curry house without getting a dish of this relish and a stack of *papads*—those wonderful, crunchy Indian crackers?

2 cups chopped onion
¼ cup fresh lime juice
1 teaspoon paprika
1 teaspoon chili powder
½ teaspoon salt
***Papads* (optional), for serving**

1. Combine the onion, lime juice, paprika, chili powder, and salt in a large bowl and mix well, until all the ingredients are evenly distributed.

2. Cover the bowl and refrigerate for at least 1 hour to allow the flavors to combine before serving. Serve at room temperature with *papads*, or as a side dish with Chicken Tikka Masala (page 110) or a curry.

onion cuisine

It kind of hits you in two stages. First, you taste a certain sweetness in a dish you have ordered at a curry shop, but you are sure it didn't come from sugar. Then, when you visit a grocery around the corner, you notice the huge quantity of onions for sale.

Soon enough you realize that everything in a curry house in Great Britain seems to be based on onions. And not just a bit of onion, but vast amounts of onions, slowly cooked until their unique taste becomes the foundation for an entire cuisine. To see this magic for yourself, whip up a batch. Heat some oil over medium-low heat in a skillet, add the onions, cook them with an occasional stir, and watch them transform. It seems as if it takes forever, but really it's just an hour. You'll have onions that are soft, a bit mushy, and somehow sweet. Slow cooking unlocks the sugar trapped inside. Too much heat just burns the onions; only low heat and time can do the job.

Many Indian dishes, even these Anglo versions, are based on the slow cooking of lots of onions. Accept it, fill your kitchen with wonderful smells, and enjoy the rewards.

Shrimp Biryani

Makes 4 servings

Even though it's not fried, biryani seems to be India's answer to fried rice. It's a great rice-based dish with those intense Indian flavors. You'll find frozen pouches of grated coconut at Indian groceries.

2 cups basmati rice
3 quarts water
2 tablespoons unsalted butter
1 tablespoon finely chopped hot green chile
1 tablespoon garam masala powder
2 bay leaves
2 tablespoons finely chopped fresh ginger
3 garlic cloves, crushed and chopped
½ cup cashew nuts
¼ cup raisins
½ cup grated coconut
1 cup chopped onion
1 pound peeled and deveined medium-size shrimp
½ cup fresh or frozen green peas
1 teaspoon salt

1. Soak the basmati rice in 2 quarts of the water for 20 minutes. Drain and set aside.

2. Melt the butter in a large heavy skillet over medium-low heat and add the chile, garam masala, and bay leaves. Cook, stirring, until the spices are coated with butter and are releasing their fragrance, about 3 minutes.

3. Add the ginger, garlic, cashews, raisins, coconut, and onions and continue cooking, stirring occasionally, until the onions become tender and translucent, about 20 minutes more.

4. Increase the heat to medium, add the shrimp and rice, and continue to cook, stirring occasionally, until the shrimp are opaque and the rice is coated with the spices, about 5 minutes.

5. Mix in the peas, salt, and remaining 1 quart of water, increase the heat to high, and boil the water for 1 minute.

6. Give the mixture one last stir, reduce the heat to low, cover the pot, and let it cook, undisturbed, until all the water has been absorbed and the rice is cooked, about 15 minutes. Remove the bay leaves and serve warm.

VARIATION: You can use brown basmati rice instead. If you do, increase the cooking time in step 6 to 40 minutes.

the hot stuff

Tyne Bridge,
Newcastle, England

Traveling northward through England, you'll notice the spice level of curries rising steadily. A dish that's mild in Bristol will be a bit more spicy in Manchester. When you reach Newcastle, well . . . consider yourself warned.

One thing you'll learn about the people of Newcastle is that their die-hard soccer fans are shirtless and done up in body paint on even the coldest, dampest days. All this makes you wonder "What keeps them warm?" Once you get there and start tasting the local food, the answer becomes obvious. They eat what have to be the spiciest curries that exist. Restaurants invite you to take "The Curry Hell Challenge" with their classic dish of fire, called *phal*.

Phal scares people. Not just the dish, but even the word itself. Yes, there are other legendary hot dishes, such as *magmaloo* and *tindaloo*, but these are served so rarely that they're almost urban myth. Phal is more of a real-life legend. It's for guys who need to show everybody how tough they are, especially when they're eating.

While phal (or phaal, as it's sometimes spelled) reaches its peak in the north of England, it also can be found in the United States at the Brick Lane Curry House, one of New York's most authentic British restaurants. There, the chef wears a gas mask while he cooks and a huge show is made of just how hot the dish is. Indeed, if you finish it, they give you a certificate.

Scottish Rabbit Curry

Makes 4 servings

Okay, rabbit is a traditional meat and curry is a classic sauce, but who knew they went together? Of course, in curry-crazy Britain, you shouldn't be surprised. Traditionally, this dish is called a Scottish curry, but it's really just a British rabbit stew with curry added.

2 tablespoons unsalted butter
1 (2- to 2½-pound) rabbit, cut into serving pieces
½ cup chopped British or Canadian bacon (see sidebar, page 91)
1 tablespoon all-purpose flour
2 tablespoons mild curry paste
3 cups low-sodium chicken broth
1½ cups pearl onions
2 cups button mushrooms
1 cup chopped celery
1 teaspoon salt
Basmatic rice (optional), for serving

1. In a Dutch oven, melt the butter over medium heat and sauté the rabbit pieces until well browned, about 15 minutes. Remove from the pan and reserve.

2. Using the same pan you browned the rabbit in, and without wiping it out, sauté the bacon over medium heat until it's browned and has rendered its fat in the pan, about 10 minutes. Add the flour and cook, whisking constantly, until it is dissolved, about 3 minutes. Add the curry paste and stir to combine well with the flour mixture. Stir in the chicken broth, ¼ cup at a time. The pan contents now will have the consistency of a thin sauce.

3. Reduce the heat to medium-low and add the browned rabbit pieces along with the onions, mushrooms, celery, and salt. Simmer the dish, stirring occasionally, until the meat is cooked through, the onions are tender, and the sauce has thickened up, about 1½ hours. Serve warm, preferably over rice.

ON *the* SIDE

M any main courses are eaten in the UK as complete meals in themselves, but plenty of side dishes show up on British tables, too. A lot of them are potato based. Peas are another favorite.

Pan Haggerty (page 126), Clapshot (page 125), and Bubble and Squeak (page 128) are creatively named potato dishes that take the universal root vegetable and make it uniquely British. The pea-based dishes, contrary to stereotype, are not garden-fresh green peas cooked to mush. They're another thing altogether: long-cooked dried peas similar to the green split peas you find on the dried-beans shelf of American supermarkets.

So cook them up. These have been the staples of generations of cooks. They are tasty ways of coping with leftovers and a reminder of what a humble starch or legume can do.

pilgrimage: to market, or maybe a couple of markets

The Borough Market in London is not a place to go in order to do your ordinary, everyday grocery shopping. And it's not like your local farmers' market either. But if you want to pick up a few raw oysters, an organic, free-range chicken, or some seasonal local produce for dinner, there is no better place.

The Borough Market combines a food court, a food market, and a social space. It's also a popular backdrop for mass media; I've never been to the market without seeing—even on days when the vendors aren't there—some kind of photo shoot or video production. The market shows off London at its best: energetic, sophisticated, bustling, and striving for excellence.

Here all the English food passions are on display. You can get seven or eight varieties of mushrooms, including wild puffballs, which I've never seen in any other market. There are meats of every sort—not just lamb, beef, chicken, and pork, but also pheasant, partridge, grouse, teal, mallard, venison, hare, and wild rabbit. (The last two looked about the same to me.) Baked goods range from flapjacks (which are different from what Americans call flapjacks; see the recipe on page 172) to cheesecake to fine French pastries.

I'm not sure if it was the giant wheels of Parmesan from Italy or the whole artisanal Stiltons from the north of England that first convinced me the Borough Market was one of the best places in the world to buy cheese. It could have been the farmhouse cheeses from Switzerland, Wales, or Holland, too. Perhaps I was most impressed by the condition of the cheeses: None had that stale, dried-out look to which supermarket cheese shoppers have grown accustomed.

As you stroll through the Borough Market, there is a bounty of prepared foods, too—some from the British Isles and others imported. Organic chocolate-walnut brownies made with spelt flour, prosciutto di Desulo from Sardinia, and candies from an Italian monastery were among the choices on one of my visits.

What you won't see at Borough Market are farmers. For that, you'll have to head, as I have, to a market like the one at Notting Hill, the London neighborhood famed for its cool shops and hip residents. Will you find movie stars choosing salad greens? Not exactly, but there were all sorts of people there who looked very creative and just as important.

Although the twenty or so stalls in the Notting Hill Market were well hidden in a courtyard parking lot, they turned out to be less than fifty yards from the Notting Hill Gate Tube station. Just follow the signs through a portico and down a wheelchair ramp, and you'll find the typical green and white awnings of farmers' markets everywhere.

While Notting Hill has the sorts of colorful vegetables and fruits Americans typically look for in a good farmers' market, about a third of the vendors were selling meat and almost as many were bakers. One stand sold eggs, which you could choose yourself, one at a time, while another offered organic offal. At another stand a beautiful piece of prime rib was being weighed out as I walked by.

Rabbit, partridge, and venison were surprisingly common.

What about that produce? Everything from purple sprouting broccoli to red torpedo onions were there and worth buying. I checked out a "punnet of organic lamb's lettuce" and bought it—just to find out what a punnet was. (It turned out to be the British word for "display container.") Bunches of carrots, heads of garlic, and basket after basket (or punnet after punnet) of peppers were being browsed by a huge crowd. Only one vendor specialized in fruit, with a stand that featured Cox, Egremont Russet, Saturn, and Bramley apples, and Comice pears. Baskets of berries were on display, too; where else was the climate just right for both berries and apples in October?

Finally, there was cheese— cow's milk, goat's milk, and even hard cheese from "buffalo milk." Thinking at first that this meant American bison, I asked how they milked them. It turned out they were water buffalo, but still quite difficult to milk. "They don't let men go near them," the woman in charge of the stand told me. A male voice in the crowd cried out, "My wife is the same way!"

Walk through the Notting Hill Market or its counterpart in Marylebone on a late summer or fall morning, and you'll see that it's all there: basics like eggs, cauliflower, apples, and pork sausages; the finer things that Londoners aspire to, like artisanal breads and farmhouse cheeses; and even luxuries like fresh scallops in their shells or fillet of venison.

Are these markets where you find the soul of London cuisine? Are they closer to the soul of London cuisine than a curry restaurant with fancy folded napkins, a pie and mash shop with tile walls and wooden benches, or a fine dining room with elegant reinventions of traditional dishes? Well, you couldn't have any of them without ingredients, and there are no better places to shop than at these London markets.

CLAPSHOT

Makes 4 servings

In New Jersey, where I live, turnips are rarely seen, and when they do show up, they're on a back shelf or stuck in a corner. In the UK, by contrast, turnips are eaten all the time, often along with or instead of potatoes. Clapshot is the classic combo of turnips with potatoes.

- 4 quarts water
- 2 tablespoons plus 1 teaspoon salt
- 3 cups chopped potato
- 3 cups chopped turnip
- 2 tablespoons chopped fresh chives
- 2 to 3 tablespoons unsalted butter
- 1 teaspoon freshly ground black pepper

1. Bring the water to a boil in a large pot over high heat. Add 2 tablespoons of the salt and the potatoes and turnips. Allow to boil for 1 minute, reduce the heat to medium-low, and simmer, uncovered, until the turnips and potatoes are very tender, about 25 minutes. Drain the vegetables and transfer them to a large bowl.

2. Mix in the chives, 2 tablespoons of the butter, the remaining 1 teaspoon salt, and the pepper and use a potato masher to work all of the ingredients into a thick paste. If the mixture is too dry, add another tablespoon of butter. Keep mashing until everything is well blended. Serve warm.

pubs

Pub is short for "public house," and that's just what pubs are, a sort of home away from home where people can meet, socialize, and have a drink. On a weekday evening in a typical residential neighborhood, local pubs will be filled with regulars. There might be a "quiz night" or other activity where patrons will battle it out for a few moments of local fame. On weekends, the place will be buzzing, often with the whole neighborhood packed in.

Even twenty years ago, when you wanted solid food in a pub, your choices were pretty much limited to flavored potato chips (known as crisps), pickled eggs, or maybe some nuts. Things have been changing, though. These days, you'll often find pubs offering real meals and, sometimes, serious cuisine.

The phrase "pub grub" has changed its meaning frequently. Once it simply meant food that was easily reheated, but today it's something just a bit fancier than American diner food: good-quality burgers, sausages, salads, and sandwiches, along with traditional British specialties like dumplings and mince, meat pies, and fish and chips. There are also "gastropubs" with much more ambitious kitchens. In many cases, these are Britain's temples of haute cuisine, and even though they're in buildings that look like pubs, they have the atmosphere of four-star restaurants and prices to match.

Is there an ideal time to visit? If you're looking to meet the locals, a weeknight might work best for you. If you're going to have only one pub meal, make it lunch on a Sunday. That's when people will be lining up for roast beef and Yorkshire pudding—and there's nothing's more British than that.

Pan Haggerty

Makes 4 servings

Don't pass this recipe by because you think you won't find a "Haggerty"! It's really nothing more than cooked potato and onion slices with cheese, and it makes a perfect vegetarian main course or a hearty side dish. This is your chance to use that mandoline you were given as a gift and never bothered to try. It will give you extra-thin slices. As for the name, it's said to be an English pronunciation of an earlier Celtic or, perhaps, French name. There was never any special pan.

3 cups thinly sliced potato
2 cups thinly sliced onion
2 tablespoons butter, plus more for the baking dish
½ teaspoon salt
½ teaspoon freshly ground black pepper
1 cup shredded cheddar cheese

1. Preheat the oven to 325°F. Butter a 9 x 13-inch baking dish well. Spread out the potatoes in a layer on the bottom of the dish. Next spread out the onions in a layer on top of the potatoes. Dot with the butter and sprinkle with salt and pepper.

2. Cover the dish (aluminum foil is fine) and bake for 1 hour, or until the onions are soft and the potatoes are tender.

3. Sprinkle the cheese over the vegetables and return the dish, uncovered, to the oven. Bake for 15 minutes more, or until the cheese is lightly browned. Let the dish cool at least 10 minutes before serving warm.

Stoke-on-Trent, England

BUBBLE *and* SQUEAK: FRIED CABBAGE, POTATOES, *and* CORNED BEEF

Makes 4 servings

Are there bubbles and does it squeak? Yes; the name comes from the sound and appearance of these ingredients as they hit a hot skillet. It's a great dish to make if you have a fridge full of typical British leftovers like cabbage, mashed potatoes, and boiled (or corned) beef. If you don't have enough leftovers on hand, a pot of boiling water and a few extra minutes will set you straight.

4 quarts water, to cook the cabbage and potatoes
½ teaspoon salt, or to your taste, plus 1 tablespoon if cooking cabbage and potatoes
2 cups chopped potatoes, cooked or fresh
2 cups chopped cabbage, cooked or fresh
1 tablespoon unsalted butter
2 cups chopped cooked boiled or corned beef (see cooking instructions, page 64)
½ teaspoon freshly ground black pepper

1. If your potatoes and cabbage are not already cooked, bring the water and 1 tablespoon of the salt to a boil over high heat. Add the potatoes, reduce the heat to medium-low, and simmer for 20 minutes, or until the potatoes are fork-tender. Remove the potatoes with a slotted spoon, reserving the water, and set aside. Repeat with the cabbage, but simmer it for only 10 minutes. Drain and set aside.

2. Melt the butter in a large skillet over medium heat. Add the beef and cook it, stirring occasionally, until the edges begin to brown, about 10 minutes.

3. Add the boiled cabbage and potato and continue cooking, stirring occasionally, until the vegetables begin to brown, too, about 20 minutes more.

4. Taste for salt. If the beef was salty enough, you won't need it; otherwise, add ½ teaspoon, or to taste. Add the pepper and stir. Serve hot.

NOTE: If you leave out the corned beef, you'll have colcannon, a classic Irish vegetable side dish.

PEASE PORRIDGE

Makes 4 servings

You know the rhyme, right?

Pease porridge hot, pease porridge cold,
Pease porridge in the pot, nine days old;
Some like it hot, some like it cold,
Some like it in the pot, nine days old.

It's a classic. Even though I don't recommend storing cooked food for nine days, the rhyme does offer a recipe: a dish made from peas that you can make ahead and serve a bunch of different ways. It's a soup, a spread, and maybe even a sauce, in addition to working as a side dish. *Pease* is just Old English for "peas."

1 cup dried green split peas
1 cup chopped British or Canadian bacon (see sidebar, page 91)
1 cup chopped onion
½ teaspoon salt
2 teaspoons Worcestershire sauce
5 cups water

1. Put the peas in a deep bowl, cover with at least 3 inches of water, and soak for at least 8 hours, or overnight. Rinse and drain the peas.

2. Combine the soaked peas, bacon, onion, salt, Worcestershire sauce, and the 5 cups water in a large soup pot over high heat and bring to a boil. Let the mixture boil for 1 minute.

3. Reduce the heat to medium-low and simmer, uncovered, stirring occasionally at the beginning and then more frequently near the end, until the mixture forms a thick paste, about 2 hours. If the porridge dries out before it is tender, add more water as often as you need to.

4. Serve hot, or cold, or in the pot, as the rhyme says. But if you want it nine days old, you should freeze it.

high-class mush

Well, there I was, standing in one of Manhattan's most exclusive Italian food boutiques, checking out a package of dried beans, priced at almost seven dollars a pound. Labeled *piselli secchi,* they were sealed with a special metal casting and boasted a label that was pretentious even by the rarefied standards of Italian artisanal producers. The beans had a familiar—and, to me, faintly British—look to them. I took them home to find out more.

After a closer examination, I realized that these were mushy peas! (Or, more properly, marrowfat peas.) They looked, tasted, and cooked up the very same way, but, bearing a fancy label from the boot-shaped country, they could be sold for triple the price. At that Italian shop, I was told that I could make something really special with those magic legumes. Once I got home, I did so: mushy peas that had not been processed and did not come out of a can.

MUSHY PEAS
Makes 4 servings

No, mushy peas aren't green peas cooked into a mush. They're something different entirely. Filled with flavor and fiber, they are a variety known as marrowfat peas, which, when cooked, burst and form a mushlike paste. British cooks always add a bit of baking soda to hasten this process. I do so in this recipe, but you don't have to. While you won't find mushy (or marrowfat) peas in your local supermarket, they're sold in just about every British and Irish specialty store in the United States.

1 cup dried marrowfat peas
¼ teaspoon baking soda
½ teaspoon salt
¼ teaspoon freshly ground black pepper
3 cups water

1. Put the peas in a deep bowl, cover with at least 3 inches of water, and soak for at least 8 hours, or overnight. Rinse and drain the peas.

2. Combine the peas with the baking soda, salt, pepper, and the 3 cups water in a heavy soup pot. Bring to a boil over high heat. Let the water boil for 3 minutes, reduce the heat to low, cover the pot, and simmer the peas, stirring occasionally, for about 1½ hours, or until they begin to burst and become pasty. Serve warm.

WELSH RAREBIT

Makes 4 servings

First, we'll dispense with the myths. One, it's not made with rabbit; and two, it's not just grilled cheese. What is it? It's a classic hot vegetarian sandwich, something good to put on toast. And it makes a nice companion for a bowl of soup or Cawl (page 71).

> 2 cups shredded cheddar cheese
> 1 tablespoon all-purpose flour
> 2 tablespoons unsalted butter
> 1 cup porter or stout
> 1 teaspoon powdered mustard
> 1 tablespoon Worcestershire sauce
> 1 teaspoon hot curry powder or paste
> 8 slices toasted rye or whole-wheat bread

1. Toss the shredded cheese and flour together in a large bowl. Make sure the cheese is evenly coated with the flour.

2. Combine the butter, porter, mustard powder, Worcestershire sauce, and curry powder in a saucepan over medium heat and bring to a simmer. Take care not to let the mixture boil.

3. Now, here's the tricky part: While stirring constantly, add the cheese to the simmering beer mixture, 1 tablespoon at a time. When a tablespoon of cheese has melted completely, and not before, add another. Continue until all the cheese is melted into the beer mixture. (If you add too much cheese at once, you'll wind up with a ball of rubbery fat!)

4. Place 2 slices of toast on each plate and pour the cheese mixture over the toast. Serve immediately. Store any leftover rarebit in a covered container in the refrigerator and reheat in your microwave.

SAVORY PIES
and BAKED GOODS

═══════════════

I s there a British dish more iconic than a steak and kidney pie? Pies of all sorts—Cockney meat pie filled with ground beef, fidget pie with bacon, and fish pie with a mashed potato crust, for example—are all staples of the British diet. And with the exception of the fish pie, each one is something delicious wrapped or covered with dough.

Savory pies are great one-dish meals, and they make terrific gifts. Bake one, bring it to a potluck or a bake sale, and watch the excitement. When people realize that the typical fillings of apple or cherry have been replaced by meat, fish, or vegetables, they feel they have the best of both worlds: a dish that's comforting and familiar as well as new and different.

pie for tea

When you say "tea," all sorts of things can come to mind: the iced tea most Americans know, the pot of brown liquid that comes with meals at Chinese restaurants, or maybe a cup of the stuff we serve to the elderly and sick. When the British say "tea," though, they have their own constellation of meanings, and not always the same ones: They might mean a mug with a tea bag, some boiling water, and a splash of milk; or a formal service with china and silver; or an entire meal. Even today, after decades of practice with British English, I can still be thrown when someone asks me, "Do you ever have pie for tea?"

Tea and *high tea* are used to describe early dinners or meal-size afternoon snacks. A British Rail menu from a while back offered the following high tea options:

Bacon, Egg, Sausage, Tomato, Fried Potatoes
or
Grilled Fish, Fried Potatoes
or
Cold Meats and Salads

Buttered Toasted Tea Cake
or
Buttered Toast
or
White and Brown Bread and Butter

Choice of assorted pastries or fruit cake
Preserves

Note that the drink called tea wasn't specified, but it was taken for granted. If you chose coffee, you had to pay a surcharge. Far from being a snack, this was something substantial, perhaps even too much to eat during a typical British train ride. It's clear that one of the many definitions of *tea* is a really big afternoon meal.

So a cup or pot of tea is filled with liquid, and the meal called *tea* is solid and need not even include the drink called tea, but it could certainly include pie. I think that if you sat down in the early evening to some meat pie and a cup of coffee, you could very well call that *tea,* too.

BRITISH HOT-WATER CRUST

Makes 1 double 9-inch pie crust

American pie crust recipes always seem to stress keeping things cold: there's ice water, chilled butter, and maybe even a chilled mixing bowl. The British—of course!—do it the other way around. They use hot water and hot milk, and they melt the fat.

4 cups all-purpose flour, plus more if needed
2 teaspoons salt
½ cup whole milk
1 cup shredded beef suet, lard, or shortening
½ cup water, plus hot water if needed

1. Sift the flour and salt together into a large heatproof bowl. Bring the milk, suet, and water to a simmer in a small saucepan. Watch it carefully to make sure it doesn't boil over, and give it a stir to keep things evenly distributed. Once the mixture comes to a boil, immediately pour it over the flour and mix until a dough starts forming, using a wooden spoon at first, but then, as it cools, your hands.

2. If the dough is too dry to roll out, add hot water, 1 tablespoon at a time, until it's workable. If it's too soggy, add more flour, again 1 tablespoon at a time, until you can roll it. Divide the dough into 2 equal parts, form each one into a ball, and flatten it into a disk. Sprinkle some flour on a work surface and use a rolling pin to roll out each disk of dough into a circle about 11 inches across and ⅛ inch thick.

3. Line a pie pan with one of the circles of dough and fill. Place the second circle of dough on top, crimp the edges, and bake according to the pie recipe.

BACON ROLY-POLY

Makes 1 roly-poly, to serve 4

When is a pie not exactly a pie? In this case, when it's rolled up like a Swiss roll, also known as a jellyroll.

1 cup chopped British or Canadian bacon (see sidebar, page 91)
1 cup chopped onion
1 teaspoon dried sage
1 teaspoon freshly ground black pepper
3 cups all-purpose flour, plus more if needed
1 tablespoon baking powder
1 teaspoon salt
1½ cups shredded beef suet or shortening
½ cup water, plus more if needed
1 large egg, lightly beaten
Liquor (page 143), for serving

1. Preheat the oven to 325°F. Combine the bacon, onion, sage, and pepper in a small bowl. Toss and make sure they are well blended. Set aside.

2. Sift the flour, baking powder, and salt together in a large bowl. Add the suet and use a pinching motion with your fingers to combine the flour and suet. Add the water and knead until you have a dough with the consistency of modeling clay. If it's too dry, add water, 1 tablespoon at a time, until it's moist enough. If it becomes too soggy or sticky, add flour, 1 tablespoon at a time, until you have a proper dough.

3. Sprinkle some flour on a work surface, put the dough on it, and roll it out into a rough 8 x 16-inch rectangle. Spread out the bacon and onion mixture evenly over the dough. Then roll it up, beginning at a short end, like a Swiss roll or jellyroll.

4. Oil a baking sheet. Place the roly-poly on the sheet and brush it with the beaten egg. Bake the roly-poly until the outside is golden brown, about 1½ hours. Let cool for 10 minutes before slicing. Serve warm, with Liquor.

Chicken, Ham, and Mushroom Pie

Makes 1 (9-inch) pie, to serve 6

A chicken pot pie? No, but it is a pie with chicken. This is a pie of the sort you find all over Britain, a savory combination of ingredients, which makes it the centerpiece of a meal.

½ cup chopped British or Canadian bacon (see sidebar, page 91)
1 cup chopped ham
1 cup chopped onion
½ teaspoon freshly ground black pepper
1 pound boneless, skinless chicken breast or thigh, cut into 1-inch pieces
2 cups chopped mushroom
¼ cup chopped fresh flat-leaf parsley
1 recipe British Hot-Water Crust (page 137)

1. Put the bacon in a large skillet over medium heat and cook it, stirring occasionally, until it begins to brown, about 5 minutes. Add the ham, onion, and pepper. Cook, stirring occasionally, until the onion is translucent, about 15 minutes.

2. Stir in the chicken and mushrooms and cook the mixture, stirring occasionally, until the mushrooms are tender, about 20 minutes. Add the parsley and toss, remove from the heat, and set aside.

3. Preheat the oven to 375°F. Line a 9-inch pie plate with the rolled-out bottom crust. Add the cooked chicken and ham mixture, and cover with the top crust. Use a fork to crimp and seal the edges and to poke some holes in the top crust so steam can escape.

4. Bake the pie until the crust is browned, about 45 minutes. Let cool at least 10 minutes before cutting into slices. Serve warm.

pie, mash, liquor, and maybe some eels, too

To old-timers, nothing says "London food" like pies, eels, mash (mashed potatoes), and the parsley gravy called *liquor*. In the hustle of the city's modern financial center, they've been gone for decades, and the places that offered them have been replaced by the same modern quick-service establishments you'll find the world over. A bit of searching, however, will tell you that while the classic plate that combines these foods is harder to find, it's still alive and well. With that in mind, I went on a tour of some of London's pie and mash shops.

On Bethnell Green Road, two of the last remaining outposts, unrelated but both called Kelly, hold their ground. My first stop was S & R Kelly at number 284. I almost walked past the very plain storefront and into a neighboring curry shop, but spotted my error at the last second. The inside was just as plain as the outside. When I ordered, I learned that the place had been in this location for 100 years. The tile walls and plain benches looked liked they'd seen the consumption of many millions of pies.

My plate was simple. It consisted of a "scrape of mash," a small, rectangular ground meat pie, and a handful of eel

pieces, all smothered with liquor (see recipe, page 143). Upon first taste, the mash and liquor seemed as plain and unseasoned as baby food, and the pie turned out to be roughly the same. But with a few dashes of salt and pepper and a splash of vinegar, the whole thing came alive. Of course I couldn't help but wonder why they didn't season the food in the first place, but I didn't dare ask.

What about the eels? Eels are tricky to cook; their skin is difficult to remove, and they're strongly flavored. At S & R Kelly they were given the same mild treatment as the pie and mash, but they had the sort of rich fish flavor you never find in more delicate varieties. If you like your fish bland, stay away. But if you're one of those people who thinks that most inexpensive fish sold today is tasteless, eel is your friend. Although it has a mixed, but mostly bad, reputation here in the States, in some other places, such as the East End of London, the opulent fish restaurants of Venice, and sushi bars just about anywhere, its fatty and flavorful flesh is venerated.

G. Kelly, at 414, is cut from the same pattern as S & R, minus the eels. Because the British feel obliged to explain anything that's asked of them, I inquired as to why they didn't serve eels. The woman behind the counter gave me a long dissertation on correct fish storage procedures. I think she was trying to tell me that she didn't want eels in her shop, or perhaps didn't want the extra cleanup. G. did have one thing that S & R failed to provide: spoons. With a soup spoon instead of a knife, I was able to easily clean up every last spec of parsley liquor from my plate.

My next stop, Tubby Isaac's, had no pies or mash. Tubby's is a stall on a corner by a university campus, the sort of place that might have been common fifty years ago. Founded in 1919 by Tubby Isaac Brenner and sold to the current owners in 1938, the stand is one of the last holdouts of a once thriving Cockney seafood culture.

closed the following day for Yom Kippur and no eel would be available for at least another 36 hours.

I ordered a medium bowl of jellied eel, splashed some of Tubby's homemade chili vinegar on top, and dug in. Although I froze for a moment at the thought of eating what appeared to be eel-flavored Jell-o, the savoriness of the fish and the coolness of the gelatin overrode my anxiety. I was hooked. Eaten with a bit of bread alongside, it was just too good. Here was the the sort of street food that would be a high point on a trip to Asia or South America. But this was London; indeed, this jellied eel truly was London.

By the time I got to Clarke's, at 46 Exmouth Market in Islington, on a small pedestrian-friendly street filled with restaurants and boutiques, I had spent the better part of a day searching for places that, as it turned out, no longer existed. Clarke's was the real deal, though. In the same location for 47 years, it oozed tradition. There they served small and large pies, scoops (not scrapes) of mash, liquor, and both stewed and jellied eels.

Despite the appealing bowl of jellied eel in the window, I decided to have my eels stewed this time, with liquor in a large bowl alongside a plate of pie, mash, and more liquor. Clarke's was the most civilized of the stops on my pilgrimage, offering napkins, knives, *and* spoons with their eat-in meals, a touch that I appreciated.

Overall, the differences among the establishments I visited were small ones. The potatoes were more or less dry, the liquor more or less creamy, and the pie crust more or less tender. All provided the same sense of old London, though. Here was food from a time when chili vinegar or hot mustard was the spiciest thing that people ate, stand-up fish snacks were pulled from local waters by your neighbors, life was slow enough that anybody had time to sit down to a hot lunch, and food traditions hadn't yet been threatened enough to be called food traditions in the first place.

I considered my order while a fellow customer, a man in one of those finely tailored English suits, stood in front of the stall and seriously worked over a large bowl of jellied eel. He seemed concerned, and soon I learned why: Tubby's would be

COCKNEY-STYLE MINCED MEAT PIE

Makes 4 (5-inch) pies, to serve 4

Hardly anything goes into these pies, but all sorts of things can go on them. Liquor, that green, parsley-based gravy; salt and pepper, of course; chili vinegar; and—a more recent development—a splash of hot sauce or ketchup. Remember, though, to warm a Cockney's heart, keep the seasoning to a minimum and serve them with mashed potatoes.

At pie-and-mash restaurants in London, they use rectangular pie pans, which are really tough to find. However, you can make excellent pies with the small, round 5-inch pie pans sold for mini pies and pot pies.

1 tablespoon vegetable oil
1½ pounds ground beef
1 teaspoon salt
1 teaspoon freshly ground black pepper
1 recipe British Hot-Water Crust (page 137)
Mashed potatoes (optional), for serving
Liquor (recipe follows), for serving

1. Preheat the oven to 325°F. Heat the oil in a large skillet over medium-high heat and add the beef, salt, and pepper. Cook, stirring occasionally and breaking up any clumps of meat, until the meat is well browned, about 15 minutes. Remove from the heat and set aside.

2. If you already have 2 balls of dough, divide each one into 4 equal portions for a total of 8. Use a rolling pin to roll 4 of the portions into circles that will be large enough to line the pie pans, with a slight overhang—about 7 inches across. Oil the pie pans and line them with the rolled-out dough. Roll the remaining 4 portions of dough into slightly smaller circles, and set aside.

3. Spoon about ½ cup of the browned meat mixture into each of the lined pie pans. Cover each pie with a circle of dough, and use a fork to crimp the edges together. Finally, poke a few holes in the top dough layer so the steam can escape.

4. Bake the pies until their top crusts are golden brown, about 1 hour. Remove from the oven and let rest for 10 minutes before serving. Serve with mashed potatoes, if you like, and Liquor.

LIQUOR: PARSLEY GRAVY

Makes 2 cups gravy

When you see a sign that reads "Pies, Mash, and Liquor," it doesn't mean an apple pie, an old TV show, and a shot of vodka. It means they're selling meat pies and mashed potatoes topped with this delicious green gravy.

3 tablespoons unsalted butter
3 tablespoons all-purpose flour
2 cups low-sodium chicken broth
1 teaspoon malt vinegar
1 cup finely chopped fresh flat-leaf parsley
½ teaspoon freshly ground black pepper
½ teaspoon salt (optional)

1. Melt the butter in a saucepan over medium-low heat. Whisk in the flour and cook, stirring constantly, until all the lumps are gone and the flour is beginning to brown, about 3 minutes Whisk in the chicken broth, a few spoonfuls at a time, until all the liquid is mixed in and you have a thick gravy.

2. Stir in the vinegar, parsley, and pepper, and make sure the ingredients are well blended. Taste for salt, and if the gravy needs it, add the ½ teaspoon.

3. Serve the Liquor warm. Besides Minced Meat Pie (page 142), it's great on Cottage Pie or Shepherd's Pie, (page 145), Bacon Roly-Poly (page 138), and all sorts of other meat and potato dishes.

LEEK PIE

Makes 1 (9-inch) pie, to serve 6

We all know about fruit pies, pot pies, and maybe meat pies, too. Why not vegetable pies? Here is one with leeks, a perfect green for the winter savory pie season.

1 tablespoon vegetable oil
6 cups coarsely chopped and rinsed leek (about 3 small bunches)
¼ cup heavy cream
1 cup shredded cheddar cheese
½ teaspoon dried thyme
¼ teaspoon ground nutmeg
½ teaspoon salt
1 recipe British Hot-Water Crust (page 137)
1 large egg, lightly beaten

1. Preheat the oven to 350°F. Heat the oil in a heavy skillet over medium heat. Add the leeks and cook them, stirring occasionally, until they become translucent, about 30 minutes.

2. Remove the pan from the heat. Combine the leeks, cream, cheese, thyme, nutmeg, and salt in a large bowl and mix well.

3. Oil a 9-inch pie pan and line the bottom with the rolled-out bottom pie crust. Fill with the leek mixture, and cover it with the remaining circle of dough. Use a fork to crimp and seal the edges and poke a few holes in the top of the pie. Brush the beaten egg evenly over the top crust.

4. Bake the pie for 40 minutes, or until the crust is golden and glossy. Let cool for 10 minutes before serving.

Padstow,
Cornwall, England

COTTAGE PIE *or* SHEPHERD'S PIE

Makes 6 servings

If you make this recipe with beef, it's cottage pie, and if you use lamb, it's shepherd's pie. Either way, there is meat on the bottom and potatoes on top. The potatoes brown and form a crust, which is what makes these "pies."

4 cups cooked potato
2 tablespoons unsalted butter, at room temperature
1 tablespoon vegetable oil
½ teaspoon dried rosemary
½ teaspoon dried thyme
½ teaspoon ground nutmeg
½ cup chopped onion
½ cup chopped carrot
1 pound ground beef or ground lamb
1 cup canned crushed tomatoes or tomato puree
½ cup fresh or frozen green peas
1 teaspoon salt
2 tablespoons Worcestershire sauce

1. Add the butter to the potatoes and mash them until they are no longer lumpy. Set them aside.

2. Preheat the oven to 425°F. Warm the oil in a large skillet over medium heat and add the rosemary, thyme, and nutmeg. Cook, stirring, until the spices are coated with oil and there are no dry spots, about 1 minute. Add the onion and carrot and continue cooking, stirring occasionally, until they begin to brown at the edges, about 10 minutes.

3. Mix in the ground beef or lamb. Cook until the meat begins to brown, stirring occasionally with a wooden spoon to prevent the meat from forming clumps, about 15 minutes. Mix in the tomato, peas, salt, and Worcestershire sauce, give the mixture a couple of stirs to make sure it's all well combined, and then remove from the heat and set aside.

4. Oil a 2-quart casserole and spread out the meat mixture over the bottom of the dish. Cover the meat with an even layer of the mashed potato. Bake, uncovered, for 45 minutes, or until the potato is just browned. Remove from the oven and let cool for 10 minutes before serving. Serve warm.

VEGETARIAN SHEPHERD'S PIE

Makes 6 servings

What do the vegetarians do when it's time for a savory pie? And what does everybody else do when it's time for a hearty side dish for an already meat-laden menu? Here's a solution: a substantial vegetarian shepherd's pie.

2 tablespoons unsalted butter, at room temperature
2 teaspoons salt
1 teaspoon freshly ground white pepper
4 cups cooked potato
1 tablespoon vegetable oil
1 cup chopped onion
1 cup chopped celery
2 tablespoons Worcestershire sauce
2 cups chopped carrot
2 cups chopped mushroom
2 cups chopped butternut squash
2 cups chopped cabbage
1 cup chopped red bell pepper

1. Add the butter, 1 teaspoon of the salt, and ½ teaspoon of the pepper to the potatoes and mash them until they are no longer lumpy. Set aside.

2. Warm the oil in a large skillet over medium heat, and add the onion, celery, and Worcestershire sauce. Cook, stirring occasionally, until the onion is tender and begins to brown at the edges, about 15 minutes. Mix in the carrot, mushroom, and squash and continue cooking until the squash is fork-tender, about 20 minutes more. Meanwhile, preheat the oven to 425°F.

3. Add the cabbage and bell pepper and the remaining 1 teaspoon salt and ½ teaspoon pepper and continue cooking until the cabbage has wilted, about 15 minutes. Remove from the heat and set aside.

4. Oil a 2-quart casserole and spread out the vegetable mixture over the bottom. Cover the vegetables with an even layer of the mashed potato. Bake, uncovered, for 45 minutes, or until the potato is just browned. Remove from the oven and let cool for 10 minutes before serving. Serve warm.

Steak *and* Kidney Pie

Makes 1 (9-inch) pie, to serve 6

When I was growing up in the United States, the sight of a whole pie always made me think "sweet with fruit inside." But when I got to England, I quickly learned that *pies* meant meat. In fancy pubs, a steak and kidney pie may be topped with puff pastry, but most of the time it's made with a hot-water crust (see recipe, page 137), giving it the look, but not by any means the taste, of an American pie. As for the kidneys themselves, you can get them at any artisanal or halal butcher.

½ cup all-purpose flour
½ teaspoon salt
¼ teaspoon freshly ground black pepper
1 pound beef chuck steak, cut into 1-inch cubes
2 tablespoons unsalted butter
1 cup chopped onion
2 cups sliced mushroom
2 tablespoons Worcestershire sauce
¼ teaspoon dried thyme
1½ cups water
1 cup chopped lamb kidney, with the tubes removed
   (about 6 kidneys)
1 recipe British Hot-Water Crust (page 137)

1. Preheat the oven to 350°F. Combine the flour, salt, and pepper in a dish and dredge the pieces of chuck steak in it. Make sure the meat is completely covered with flour.

2. Melt the butter in a Dutch oven over medium heat and add the chuck steak. Cook, turning the pieces frequently, until the meat is golden brown on all sides, about 8 minutes. Remove the steak pieces with a slotted spoon and set them aside.

3. Add the onion, mushroom, Worcestershire sauce, and thyme to the same pot. Cook, stirring occasionally, until the onion begins to turn brown at the edges, about 10 minutes.

4. Stir in the water and bring to a boil. Let it boil for 1 minute, return the browned beef to the pot, and lower the heat. Simmer, covered, stirring occasionally, for about 20 minutes, or until the meat is fork-tender. Stir in the kidney pieces and simmer for 1 minute more. Remove from the heat.

5. Place the rolled-out bottom pie crust in a well-oiled 9-inch pie pan. Fill with the steak and kidney mixture and lay the top crust over it. Crimp the edges shut with a fork, and poke some holes in the top crust so steam can escape. Bake for 40 minutes, or until the crust is a deep golden brown. Let cool for 10 minutes more before serving. Serve warm.

MUTTON *or* LAMB PIE

Makes 1 (9-inch) pie, to serve 6

Mutton was once a staple meat not just in Britain but also in much of the world. These days, though, mutton has gotten such a nasty rap that it can be almost impossible to find. What can you do? Substitute lamb for the moment, but keep your eyes peeled for mutton. When you find some real mutton, bring it home and make another pie.

1 tablespoon olive oil
1 cup chopped onion
1½ pounds lamb or mutton stew meat, diced
½ teaspoon salt
½ teaspoon freshly ground black pepper
1 tablespoon Worcestershire sauce
½ teaspoon ground mace
1 recipe British Hot-Water Crust (page 137)
¼ cup low-sodium beef broth

1. Preheat the oven to 325°F. Heat the oil in a large skillet over medium heat, add the onion, and cook, stirring occasionally, until it begins to brown at the edges, about 10 minutes.

2. Mix in the lamb, salt, pepper, Worcestershire sauce, and mace. Cook, stirring occasionally, until the meat is well browned, about 20 minutes. Set aside.

3. Oil a 9-inch pie pan and line it with the rolled-out bottom crust. Fill with the meat mixture. Pour the beef stock over the meat and cover with the top crust. Use a fork to crimp and seal the edges, and poke some holes in the top so steam can escape.

4. Bake the pie until the crust is browned, about 1 hour. Remove from the oven and let stand for about 10 minutes before serving. Serve warm.

FIDGET PIE

Makes 1 (9-inch) pie, to serve 6

How many ways are there to eat bacon? I believe the people who can do the best job of answering that question are the British. They enjoy bacon for breakfast and bacon sandwiches at various times of the day, and they invented the Bacon Roly-Poly (page 138) and this bacon pie. For the cider, you can use a hard (alcoholic) cider, if you like.

> **2 cups chopped British or Canadian bacon (see sidebar, page 91)**
> **2 cups chopped onion**
> **2 cups chopped Granny Smith apple**
> **2 tablespoons chopped fresh flat-leaf parsley**
> **½ teaspoon salt**
> **½ teaspoon freshly ground black pepper**
> **½ cup apple cider**
> **½ teaspoon cornstarch**
> **1 recipe British Hot-Water Crust (page 137)**
> **1 large egg, lightly beaten**

1. Preheat the oven to 325°F. Combine the bacon, onion, apple, parsley, salt, and pepper in a large bowl. Mix well. In another bowl, stir together the cider and cornstarch until the cornstarch is completely dissolved.

2. Line a 9-inch pie pan with the rolled-out bottom crust. Fill with the bacon and apple mixture. Pour the cider-cornstarch mixture over the filling, and lay the second crust on top. Crimp and seal the edges with a fork, poke a few holes in the top so steam can escape, and brush with the beaten egg.

3. Bake until the crust is golden brown, about 1 hour. Remove from the oven and let cool for about 10 minutes before slicing. Serve warm.

out west

In Britain, you'll often hear mention of "The West Country," a less-built-up and wilder place a few hundred miles due west of London. It's defined by two counties, Cornwall and Devon, which share one of the world's great seacoasts and offer hiking, water sports, and seafood for those who are willing to make the six-hour trip from London.

While most visitors will confine themselves to fishing, strolling, and dining, the tough can enjoy the area's rocky beaches, watching in awe as locals sun themselves on spectacular rock formations or staring as teens frolic in the waves with water temperatures just above freezing.

The entire shore is linked by the Southwest Coast Path, one of the world's great hiking trails. And though the locals will tell you that there isn't much public transit, there's enough: flights to Newquay, Plymouth, and Exeter; trains from London and Birmingham to Penzance, with plenty of stops and branch lines along the way; and at least a few buses a day that connect smaller villages with these gateway towns.

The West Country is knit together by a single food: the pasty, which is made of meat, vegetables, or some combination of these, wrapped in pie dough, and baked. A sack of pasties; a stupendous spot overlooking a lighthouse, castle, or village by the sea; a stiff ocean breeze; and some hot tea to warm your bones—that's the essence of the West Country.

Newlyn, Cornwall, England

FISH PIE *with* MASHED POTATO CRUST

Makes 1 (9-inch) pie, to serve 6

A fish pie is a real classic; it calls for at least two kinds of fish, shrimp, and a potato crust. This version is so popular in Cornwall that it can almost be thought of as a regional specialty.

2 cups whole milk
8 ounces salmon fillet
8 ounces tilapia, cod, or pollock fillets
8 ounces medium-size shrimp, peeled and deveined
2 hard-cooked large eggs, chopped
2 tablespoons unsalted butter
2 tablespoons all-purpose flour
¼ cup finely chopped fresh flat-leaf parsley
1 teaspoon salt, plus more for seasoning potatoes
½ teaspoon freshly ground black pepper, plus more for seasoning potatoes
6 cups mashed russet or Yukon gold potatoes (about 5 medium-size potatoes)
2 tablespoons grated Parmesan cheese

1. Preheat the oven to 325°F. In a large pot, bring the milk to a simmer over medium-low heat and add the salmon and cod. If the fish pieces fall apart, don't worry. Cook, stirring occasionally, for about 15 minutes, or until the fish is opaque. Add the shrimp and continue to cook until they are bright orange, about 2 minutes more.

2. Remove the fish and shrimp with a slotted spoon, and reserve the milk for the sauce. In a large bowl, break up the fish into flakes with a fork, checking to make sure there are no bones. Chop up the shrimp and add to the bowl. Mix in the chopped egg.

3. Make the sauce: Melt the butter in a skillet over medium-low heat. Whisk in the flour. Cook, whisking frequently, until the flour just starts to turn golden, about 5 minutes. Reduce the heat to low and add the reserved milk, a little bit at a time, whisking all the while to make sure it is incorporated without lumps. Mix in the parsley, salt, and pepper, and remove from the heat.

4. To assemble the dish, spread the fish and egg mixture on the bottom of a 9 x 13-inch glass baking dish. Pour the sauce over it. Cover with the potatoes, spreading them out into a thick layer on top. Sprinkle the top with the Parmesan and with salt and pepper to taste.

5. Bake the pie for 40 minutes, or until the top begins to brown. Let rest for 10 minutes, and then serve warm.

pilgrimage: pasties

When I started asking around for directions to the Chough Bakery, in the town of Padstow, in Cornwall, I tried a number of different pronunciations, such as the *Choo,* the *Chow,* and the *Cough* Bakery. None worked. Finally, I stumbled upon *Chuff,* which was right. The Chough is run by Elaine Ead, a pasty expert, defender, and evangelist. I was counting on Elaine to help me learn to make a great pasty.

Padstow is considered by many to be the gastronomic heart of Cornwall. Pasties are everywhere there. On the cool, gray Tuesday in October when I visited, Padstow was filled with people and pasties.

Chain outlets, snack bars, restaurants, and bakeries like Elaine's were all offering them. Here the expectations from pasty lovers run very high, and the vendors aim to exceed them.

Elaine and her daughter Louisa stressed the importance of handcrafting pasties with fresh ingredients—fresh turnips, onions, potatoes, and beef. By handcrafting they didn't mean using fancy ways of folding and sealing the dough packages, which was what I expected, but instead, carefully filling a pasty in layers, rather than with a heap of filling.

In their kitchen, the Eads demonstrated some classic techniques. They spread out potatoes, turnips, rutabagas, onions, and beef in layers over a very thin circle of dough, sealed the dough into a half-moon, and then covered the dough with a bit of egg wash. They said it was important that nothing be precooked. When all the ingredients are cooked from their raw state inside their pastry case, they take on a unique and special flavor.

Elaine emphasized that each pasty should provide the elements of an entire meal. "There's your veg, your protein, your starch, all in there," she said. This was not the case with most of the pasties I'd eaten before. Clearly, though, it could be done and was a goal worth working toward.

What could go in a pasty? There were some pretty strong opinions about this! Some people said you should never include fish. But Louisa pointed out that in times when beef was too expensive, people surely did use fish. Elaine had her own rule: no carrots. Chough's fillings included steak; steak and Stilton; chicken and mushroom; lamb, leek, and mint; cheese, leek, and onion; and mixed vegetable. They experiment with other flavors and have even

tried turkey and cranberry at Christmas. Other bakers around Padstow offered such fillings as apple rhubarb and "full English breakfast," meaning egg, bacon, and sausage.

At lunchtime, I strolled the harbor, drifting from pasty shop to pasty shop, sampling as I went along. A pasty filled with spicy chickpeas tasted like a malformed samosa. Rick Stein, the culinary godfather of Padstow, offered a haddock pasty, the only one filled with fish that I saw anywhere in town. Even though it was my fifth or sixth of the day, I bought one and ate it. The fish inside was deliciously smoked.

I developed a strategy for choosing pasties. I avoided crusts that were too flaky, almost like phyllo dough. On the other hand, if the crust looked like pie crust, I was more likely to try it. If customers were lined up, that meant turnover was high, a positive sign—unlike strange fillings, which indicated the pasty maker needed something other than quality to attract customers.

A couple of hours by bus from Padstow but still in Cornwall, I visited a town called The Lizard, which wasn't much of a gourmet destination. This southernmost point in England had a café, two pubs, a fish-and-chip joint,

and a legendary pasty shop. On my two earlier visits, the pasty shop was closed.

What was the shop called? That's a more complicated question than you'd expect. A sign by the bus stop pointed to "Ann's Famous Pasties," while another sign directed me to "Anne's Pasties." The banner over the front door read, "The Lizard Pasty Shop." But there was only one pasty shop in town.

On this visit the shop was open. There were only two choices: Steak was one, cheese the other. No "bacon, haddock, carrot, and Stilton" here! I ordered a medium steak. Ann(e)'s crew knew

they had it right. There was far less meat and dough than in the Padstow pasties I had sampled, and therefore proportionately more vegetables, potato and carrot. Without the giant seam of crust at the edges, the flavor of the filling shone through.

I wanted to eat another pasty or two, but while I was standing out front and chatting with the other customers, the shop closed. It was the middle of the afternoon and more customers were arriving steadily, but the door was suddenly locked. Less than an hour, and only one pasty later, I was on the next bus out of town.

TRADITIONAL CORNISH STEAK PASTY

Makes 12 pasties, to serve 6

Everybody who has been to western England has tried a pasty, that turnover of meat, vegetables, and almost anything else local shopkeepers can think of. Many pasties are mass produced, but the better shops make them by hand (see page 154). Here's a recipe for a traditional handmade one.

2 recipes British Hot-Water Crust (page 137)
2 cups chopped potato
2 cups chopped onion
2 cups chopped turnip
1 pound skirt steak, diced (¼-inch dice)
1 tablespoon salt
1 tablespoon freshly ground black pepper
1 large egg, lightly beaten

1. Preheat the oven to 325°F. If you have 2 balls of dough, divide each one into 6 equal portions, for a total of 12, and roll each into a ball. Dust a work surface with flour and use a rolling pin to roll each ball into a circle about 6 inches in diameter and a scant ⅛ inch thick. (Use a bowl or a very large cookie cutter as a template if you like.)

2. Leaving a ½-inch border for folding and sealing, cover half of each circle with a layer of potato. In layers add the onion, turnip, and beef, so that each layer covers the one below it. Sprinkle the filling with salt and pepper.

3. Fold the border of dough over the filling and pinch the dough repeatedly to create a seam that runs from end to end across the side of each pasty. If you want something a bit fancier, you can roll the seam or even try a twisted edge. Place the pasties on a well-oiled baking sheet, use a fork to poke a few holes in the top so steam can escape, and brush the pasties with the beaten egg.

4. Bake the pasties until the crusts are well browned, about 1 hour. Let rest for 10 minutes before serving.

YORKSHIRE PUDDING

Makes 12 individual puddings

The first time I ate a Yorkshire pudding, I realized that, well, it wasn't the first time at all. It prodded my memory and teased me a bit before I reached far enough back to recall what it was that was just so similar. It was the popovers that my mom, who had never been to England and had never read a foreign cookbook, baked all the time.

Food writers spill a lot of ink describing the "proper" way to eat Yorkshire puddings. But there are a lot of different ideas about this. What most people agree on is that there should be a roast and gravy somewhere nearby.

1½ cups bread flour
1 teaspoon salt
4 large eggs
1½ cup whole milk

1. Preheat the oven to 400°F. Combine the flour, salt, eggs, and milk in a large bowl. Beat until all the lumps are gone and a thick, creamy batter has formed.

2. Oil a 12-cup muffin pan and pour the batter into the cups. Bake until the tops are golden brown, about 20 minutes. Do not open the oven during the baking time, or the puddings will collapse. Serve warm with a roast. Beef is traditional, but they're great with turkey or pork, too.

GARDEN VEGETABLE PASTY

Makes 12 pasties, to serve 6

Sometimes you can make a vegetarian version of a dish just by removing the meat. At other times, you may want to reinvent the dish to showcase new ingredients or techniques. This pasty uses traditional methods, but it's certainly not a traditional pasty.

2 recipes British Hot-Water Crust (page 137)
1 cup chopped onion
1 cup chopped turnip
½ cup chopped carrot
1 cup chopped broccoli
1 cup chopped mushroom
1 cup chopped potato
1 cup fresh or frozen peas
1 teaspoon salt
½ teaspoon freshly ground black pepper
2 tablespoons Worcestershire sauce
1 large egg, lightly beaten

variations on the pasty

The two pasty recipes here are common, but you don't have to limit yourself. In a traditional Cornish pasty made with meat (page 156), beef is the norm, but you can use chicken breast, pork loin, lamb, or even salmon fillet. For the Garden Vegetable Pasty, you can mix, match, and replace ingredients to your taste. You could use corn instead of peas, for example, or spinach instead of broccoli. Just make sure you start with a base of potato pieces on the bottom.

1. Preheat the oven to 325°F. If you have 2 balls of dough, divide each one into 6 equal portions, for a total of 12, and roll each into a ball. Dust a work surface with flour and use a rolling pin to roll out each ball into a circle about 6 inches in diameter and a scant ⅛ inch thick.

2. Leaving a ½-inch border for folding and sealing, cover half of each circle with a layer of potato. Combine the onion, turnip, carrot, broccoli, and mushroom in a large bowl and toss or stir to distribute evenly. Cover the potato with the vegetable mixture, and layer the peas on top. Sprinkle the filling with some of the salt, pepper, and Worcestershire sauce.

3. Fold the dough over the filling and pinch the dough repeatedly to create a seam that runs from end to end across the side of each pasty. If you want something a bit fancier, you can roll the seam or even try a twisted edge.

4. Place the pasties on a well-oiled baking sheet, use a fork to poke a few holes in the top so steam can escape, and brush with the beaten egg.

5. Bake the pasties until the crusts are well browned, about 1 hour. Let rest for 10 minutes before serving.

TOAD-IN-THE-HOLE

Makes 4 servings

If the British ate roasted toad, they'd probably call it sausage. After all, the name of their classic sausage dish was inspired by the toad.

> 1 tablespoon vegetable oil
> 4 large Italian sweet or English-style pork sausages (about 1½ pounds)
> 1 recipe Yorkshire Pudding (page 159), prepared through step 1

1. Preheat the oven to 400°F. Warm the oil in a skillet over medium-high heat, add the sausages, and cook, stirring occasionally, until the casings are well browned, about 10 minutes. Remove from the heat and set aside.

2. Oil a 9 x 13-inch baking dish and pour the Yorkshire Pudding batter into it. Add the sausages. Bake until the batter has risen and browned, about 25 minutes. Let cool for 10 minutes and serve warm.

The
SWEET SIDE

C ollectively, the people of Great Britain have one serious sweet tooth. From the candy bar that comes with most airline meals to the swoon-inducing cakes offered in tea shops all over the country, sweets are universally loved. With British sweets, names can fool you. Poor Knights of Windsor (page 180) are what we would call French toast, and Flapjacks (page 172), which are more like granola bars, don't resemble our pancakes at all. Of course there's always Spotted Dick (page 181), the steamed pudding that isn't like any other food anywhere.

pilgrimage: deep-fried candy bars

One recipe you won't find in this book is deep-fried candy bars. Yes, people enjoy them all over Britain. It's just that I couldn't bring myself to make them. I was not exactly unwilling to try them on their home turf, but the concentration of fat and calories made me tremble with fear. Nonetheless, I toughened up one day and headed to the Carron Fish Bar in Stonehaven, Scotland, the establishment that claims to be the birthplace of deep-fried candy bars.

What might I have been afraid of? Is any food that's not labeled "diet" or "healthy" dangerous? Yes, deep-fried candy bars must

be really fattening, but lots of other foods are, too, and most of them don't scare me. And it was the sort of folk food I normally would revel in. A deep-fried candy bar could be washed down with a cup of hot tea and walked off with an afternoon stroll.

For the past twenty-odd years, the Carron (formerly the Haven) has been serving its famous deep-fried Mars bars. While I was the first to tell the staff of the snack's popularity in Brooklyn, New York, they had been seeing people from all over the world wandering in to their shop for a taste.

Soon Doug, the man who

claimed to be the inventor, was pulling a Mars bar out of the fridge, splashing it with water so flour would stick, dipping it in batter, and frying away, while Kelsey, a young woman who also worked in the shop, was bouncing around with excitement. After a few minutes, I was handed what looked like a single frozen-fish stick on a plate. It was my deep-fried Mars bar. I paid for it, one pound even, and headed across the street to a public space, where I could eat and also photograph the exterior of the bar.

It should go without saying that the deep-fried Mars bar didn't care what anybody thought of it. It had a flavor and life of its own: layers of warm chocolate, a crispy crust, and rivulets of brown goo seeping through. I took one bite and fell in love.

Like haggis, it's a Scottish dish that's been misrepresented. If this were presented to you in a fine restaurant in New York or London, you'd be delighted to try it. I can almost hear the raves: about the way the different layers

of chocolate mix, about the contrast between the crisp surface and the molten interior (I think I stole that line from a real restaurant review somewhere), and about how the combination of its components was a tour de force of molecular gastronomy.

After I finished, I strolled around Stonehaven for a while. It was a collection of mostly modern buildings on a pleasant enough harbor. It did not make for a high-priority destination for American tourists—unless, of course, they wanted one of those deep-fried Mars bars from the original source.

So why no recipe? Well, to get it right, you've got to devote three or four quarts of frying oil to the task. It didn't seem worth it.

BAKED JAM ROLY-POLY

Makes 1 roly-poly, to serve 4

To Americans, a roly-poly looks like a giant version of a Swiss roll or jellyroll. But to the British, it's a classic comfort food. This one, filled with strawberry jam, is a perfect snack or dessert.

3 cups all-purpose flour, plus more if needed
1 tablespoon baking powder
¼ teaspoon salt
1 tablespoon sugar
1½ cups beef suet or shortening
½ cup water, plus more as needed
1 cup strawberry jam or fruit preserves

1. Preheat the oven to 325°F. Sift together the flour, baking powder, salt, and sugar in a large bowl. Add the suet and use a pinching motion with your fingers to combine with the flour until fully mixed. The texture should be sandy, like bread crumbs. Add the water and knead until you have a dough that is about the consistency of modeling clay. If the dough is too dry, add water, 1 tablespoon at a time, until it's moist enough. If it becomes too soggy or sticky, add flour, 1 tablespoon at a time, until you have a proper dough.

2. Sprinkle some additional flour on a work surface. Turn the dough out onto it, and roll out into a 9 x 18-inch rectangle. Spread the jam on the dough in a thin, even layer. Then roll up the dough, beginning at a short end, like a Swiss roll.

3. Oil a baking sheet and transfer the roly-poly to it. Bake the roly-poly until the outside is golden brown, about 1½ hours. Let it cool 10 minutes, then slice 1 inch thick. Serve warm with coffee or tea. A bit of Custard Sauce (page 168) would be a special treat.

CUMBERLAND PUDDING

Makes 6 servings

Steamed puddings are a unique feature of British cooking. Essentially, they're unbaked pastries. And that gives them an extra-rich and distinctive texture.

- 1 cup all-purpose flour
- ½ teaspoon baking powder
- 1 cup fresh, unflavored bread crumbs
- ½ teaspoon salt
- ½ cup beef suet or shortening
- 1 cup chopped apple
- ½ cup currants
- ½ cup packed light brown sugar
- 2 teaspoons grated lemon zest
- 3 tablespoons chopped candied orange peel
- 2 large eggs
- ½ cup granulated sugar
- ¼ teaspoon ground nutmeg
- 1 tablespoon cornstarch
- 1 cup boiling water
- 2 tablespoons fresh lemon juice

1. Mix the flour, baking powder, bread crumbs, and salt together in a large bowl. Add the suet and use a pinching motion with your fingers to combine it with the flour mixture. You should have a mixture that looks a bit sandy.

2. Use your hands to mix in the apple, currants, brown sugar, 1 teaspoon of the lemon zest, the orange peel, and eggs and work it all by hand into a dough. If the mixture is too dry, add water 1 tablespoon at a time, until a soft dough forms.

3. Butter the inside of a 6-cup heatproof glass bowl, put the dough in it, and cover it with foil.

4. To steam the bowl of pudding dough, pour about 1 inch of water into a large pot, place the bowl of dough in a steamer basket, and put it into the pot. If you don't have a steamer basket that big, put a large cookie cutter or metal trivet in the pot and put the bowl on top. Cover the pot, and place it over medium heat. Let the pudding steam in simmering water for 2 hours. Check the pot every 20 minutes or so to make sure there's enough water, and add more if needed. At the end of the cooking time, the pudding should be firm all the way through.

5. Meanwhile, make the sauce: Combine the granulated sugar, nutmeg, and cornstarch in a saucepan over low heat. Slowly add the boiling water, stirring constantly, until you have a smooth liquid with no lumps. Then add the lemon juice and the remaining 1 teaspoon lemon zest. Mix well one more time, and set aside.

6. After the pudding has finished steaming, remove it from the pot and let it cool for 10 minutes in the bowl. Unmold the pudding onto a plate. Slice it, spoon the sauce over it, and serve warm.

CUSTARD SAUCE

Makes 2 cups

Does this custard sauce look familiar? There are similar ones in Italy and France, but their cuisines don't have dishes with whimsical names like Spotted Dick (page 181) or Baked Jam Roly-Poly (page 165) to go under them.

6 large egg yolks
1 teaspoon cornstarch
3 tablespoons superfine sugar
¼ teaspoon salt
½ teaspoon pure vanilla extract
2 cups heavy cream

1. Whisk together the egg yolks, cornstarch, sugar, salt, and vanilla in a large bowl. Make sure the mixture is smooth and well blended. It may take a minute or two.

2. Bring a couple of inches of water to a simmer in the bottom of a double boiler, pour the cream into the top, and heat the cream, keeping it just below a simmer.

3. Add a third of the cream to the egg mixture, 1 table-spoon at a time, whisking constantly. The trick here is to whisk the mixture fast enough to make sure the eggs don't scramble.

4. Whisking constantly again, return the egg-cream mixture to the remaining cream in the top of the double boiler. Whisk over medium-low heat until the custard thickens, about 15 minutes. Serve warm. If you make it ahead, store it in the refrigerator and reheat in the double boiler.

BANOFFEE PIE

Makes 1 (9-inch) pie, to serve 6

Banoffee pie—its name is a contraction of *banana* and *toffee*—is one of those pies that would fit right in at a Midwestern farm-town coffee shop. Yet the British have embraced it and made it their own, and they even make banoffee-flavored ice cream.

2 cups sweetened condensed milk
¼ teaspoon salt
1½ cups graham cracker crumbs
¼ cup packed dark brown sugar
½ teaspoon ground nutmeg
8 tablespoons (1 stick) unsalted butter, melted
3 cups sliced bananas (about 2 whole bananas)
2 cups whipped cream, for serving

1. Preheat the oven to 425°F. Combine the condensed milk and the salt in an ovenproof dish, cover it tightly, and place the dish in a roasting pan. Put the roasting pan with the dish into the oven, and then add enough water to the pan so it almost reaches the top of the dish (be sure to keep the water from sloshing inside the dish). Bake until the milk is well browned, about 2 hours, checking every 30 minutes or so to make sure the water level is high enough. (If too much of the water evaporates, the milk will scorch.) Set aside and let cool to room temperature. The pie will need no further baking.

2. Combine the graham cracker crumbs, brown sugar, nutmeg, and melted butter in a large bowl. Use your hands to mix until a dough forms.

3. Butter a 9-inch pie pan, and then press the dough evenly into the bottom and sides of the pie pan so that it forms a crust. Let it firm up for at least 1 hour in the refrigerator.

4. Spoon the baked milk (now called toffee) over the pie crust and mix the banana slices evenly through it. Chill in the refrigerator for at least 1 hour so the filling can set properly. Cover evenly with the whipped cream, and serve right away.

FAT RASCALS

Makes 6 to 8 large cookies

I heard about fat rascals long before I tasted them. In the interim, I tried to imagine what would go into a cookie by that name. My mind raced with images of cream, chocolate, caramel, and other rich dessert ingredients. But when the time came to bake them, eat them, and write a recipe, I learned that *fat* meant lard. And lard is what you want for the flakiest texture. You can, however, use shortening if you prefer.

2 cups all-purpose flour
1 teaspoon baking powder
1 cup packed dark brown sugar
¾ cup currants
¼ teaspoon salt
1 teaspoon ground cinnamon
¼ teaspoon ground cloves
1 cup lard or shortening
½ cup whole milk
¼ cup granulated sugar

1. Preheat the oven to 325°F. Mix together the flour, baking powder, brown sugar, currants, salt, cinnamon, and cloves in a large bowl.

2. Combine the flour mixture with the lard, using your fingers to pinch the ingredients together until a dough begins to form. Add the milk, 1 tablespoon at a time, until the dough has the consistency of modeling clay.

3. Sprinkle your work surface with some additional flour and roll the dough out into a sheet ½ inch thick. (Yes, these are fat cookies.) Then use a 2- or 3-inch round cookie cutter to cut out disks.

4. Grease a baking sheet with butter, lard, or shortening. Place the cookies 2 inches apart on the baking sheet and bake them until they are golden brown, about 25 minutes. Sprinkle them with the granulated sugar and return them to the oven for 5 minutes more. Remove from the oven, let cool, and serve.

FLAPJACKS

Makes 6 bars

Somehow, the word *flapjack* has become the name for two different foods. Order a plate of flapjacks in the States and you'll get pancakes; order a plate of flapjacks in the UK and you'll get something that looks like a granola bar made with oats. It's a classic teatime snack.

> 8 tablespoons (1 stick) unsalted butter, melted
> ½ cup packed dark brown sugar
> ½ cup granulated sugar
> ½ cup unsweetened shredded coconut
> ½ cup honey
> 2 cups rolled oats
> 1 cup crushed mixed nuts
> 1 cup raisins

1. Preheat the oven to 325°F. Use a wooden spoon to stir the melted butter, brown sugar, granulated sugar, coconut, honey, oats, nuts, and raisins together in a large bowl. You will have a thick, sticky dough. Make sure that all the ingredients are evenly distributed.

2. Line a 9-inch square baking dish with parchment paper. Oil it, and then dust it with all-purpose flour. Spoon the dough into the lined pan.

3. Bake until the top is well browned, about 1 hour. As soon as you remove the hot pan from the oven, cut the dough into 6 equal rectangular bars. Set aside and let cool a bit before removing the cut bars from the pan. Serve warm. If they harden, reheat them in the oven, and they'll soften right up.

FRUIT TRIFLE

Makes 4 servings

This is called a trifle, yet there's nothing trifling about it at all. With layers of cake, fruit, and cream, it's a serious dessert. If you're serving grownups only, you can substitute whiskey or rum for the pineapple juice if you like.

- 4 cups cubed pound cake (1-inch cubes)
- 1 cup strawberry preserves
- 1 cup pineapple juice
- 1 recipe Custard Sauce (page 168)
- 1 cup mixed fresh or frozen berries, such as strawberries and raspberries
- 2 tablespoons unsweetened shredded coconut
- 2 cups whipped cream, for serving

1. Spread at least one side of each of the pound cake pieces with strawberry preserves and put the pieces in a large glass bowl. Spoon or pour any remaining preserves on top. Pour the pineapple juice over the cake pieces.

2. Spread the custard sauce evenly over the cake and preserves. Then spread the berries over the custard sauce and sprinkle with the coconut. Let the whole thing set, covered with plastic wrap, in the refrigerator for at least 1 hour.

3. To serve, spoon some of the trifle onto each dessert plate and cover with whipped cream.

the tea tray

All sorts of things distinguish great bed-and-breakfast rooms from sad ones, but there's one thing that will always make the intrepid traveler in Great Britain happy—an exceptional tea tray. That means a tray in your room with a hot-water kettle, a few cups, instant beverages, and some sort of snack. The best tea trays will include a pitcher of fresh cream, good tea bags, coffee, and hot cocoa, cookies (called biscuits, of course), chocolate mints, and maybe even that small touch of British food love, a candy bar.

Only once did I ever have a B & B room that lacked both a tea tray and a television. At first, I thought I might have been ripped off. Then, when I went down to the lounge and flipped on the "guest TV," the owner came out and said, "You haven't asked for tea! Let me get you some." He came out with a pot of tea and lots of toast, butter, jam, cookies, and even a Kit Kat. By the time the weather forecast was over, I was too full to eat dinner.

SPICY GINGERSNAPS

Makes 24 cookies

Ginger is a savory flavor in most of the world, yet when it came to Europe, it found its way into sweets. Gingersnaps, also known in the UK as ginger biscuits and ginger nuts, are the cookie cousin of gingerbread, and a favorite of mine. I've encountered this interpretation, with cayenne pepper, ginger, and cloves, a number of times in Great Britain.

2½ cups all-purpose flour
2 teaspoons baking soda
1 teaspoon ground cinnamon
1 tablespoon ground ginger
1 teaspoon ground cayenne pepper
1 teaspoon ground cloves
½ teaspoon salt
8 tablespoons (1 stick) unsalted butter, at room temperature
1 cup packed light brown sugar
2 tablespoons unsulphured molasses
1 large egg
2 tablespoons grated fresh ginger

1. Preheat the oven to 325°F. Sift together the flour, baking soda, cinnamon, ground ginger, cayenne, cloves, and salt in a large bowl. Set aside.

2. Cream the butter and brown sugar together in a separate bowl with a wooden spoon. Then add the molasses, egg, and fresh ginger, stirring until you have a smooth batter.

3. Stir the flour mixture into the butter and sugar, ¼ cup at a time. Make sure each addition is well blended before you add more.

4. Butter a baking sheet. Form the dough into 1-inch balls, and press them into disks about ¼ inch thick. Place them on the baking sheet with at least 1 inch between them. Bake for 20 minutes, or until the gingersnaps are golden brown. Let cool before serving.

HOT CROSS BUNS

Makes 8 buns

I remember singing the song "Hot Cross Buns" as a child. But it wasn't until I was an adult that I realized they were a food. They originated as an Easter specialty (hence the cross, of course), but now are eaten all year round. English superstition holds that hot cross buns taken on a ship will protect it from sinking. I haven't tried this myself, though.

4 cups all-purpose flour, plus more if needed
1 packet instant yeast (about 2¼ teaspoons)
3 tablespoons light brown sugar
1¾ cups whole milk, plus more if needed
4 tablespoons (½ stick) unsalted butter, melted
1 large egg, lightly beaten
1 teaspoon ground cinnamon
½ teaspoon ground nutmeg
½ teaspoon ground allspice
¼ teaspoon ground cloves
¼ teaspoon ground ginger
½ cup currants
¼ cup candied lemon peel
1 cup confectioners' sugar
½ teaspoon pure vanilla extract
1 teaspoon fresh lemon juice

1. Combine the flour, yeast, brown sugar, 1½ cups of the milk, butter, egg, cinnamon, nutmeg, allspice, cloves, and ginger in a large bowl. Using first a spoon and then your hands, blend these ingredients together until they form a wet dough. If the dough is too dry, add more milk, 1 tablespoon at a time, until the dough is moist and no longer cracks while you're kneading. If it's too soggy to knead, add flour, 1 tablespoon at a time, until you have dough that holds together well enough to knead.

2. Sprinkle some additional flour on a work surface and spread the dough out in a sort of flat pancake shape, about ¼ inch thick. Then spread the currants and lemon peel over the top. Fold the dough in half so that the fruit is on the inside, and then fold in half again. Knead the dough until it becomes elastic, about 5 minutes. When you push your thumb into the dough, the imprint from your thumb should bounce right back.

3. Oil a large bowl and place the dough in it. Cover with a tea towel and put in a warm, draft-free place. Leave it there until the dough doubles in size, about 2 hours.

4. Punch down the dough by kneading for a few seconds more. Then divide the dough into 8 equal parts. Roll each piece of dough into a ball and place the balls on a well-oiled baking sheet, about 3 inches apart. Cover with a towel and let them double in size again, about 2 hours more.

5. While the dough is rising, preheat the oven to 375°F, and make the glaze: Combine the confectioners' sugar, vanilla, and lemon juice with the remaining ¼ cup milk in a saucepan over low heat. Stir gently as the mixture heats. When the sugar is dissolved and you have a syrup, set aside.

6. Use a sharp knife to cut a cross in the top of each ball of dough. Bake the buns until the tops just begin to brown, about 20 minutes.

7. Remove from the oven and brush some of the glaze over each bun, following the two directions of the cross. Return the buns to the oven and bake until deeply browned, about 15 minutes more. Serve warm.

MINCEMEAT CAKE

Makes 1 (9-inch) round cake, to serve 6

On a chilly afternoon, nothing is better with a hot cup of tea than the sweet and spicy flavors of a cake like this one. Look for prepared mincemeat in the baking supplies section of your supermarket. Despite the name, modern mincemeat contains no meat or animal products.

1 cup all-purpose flour
1 teaspoon baking soda
½ teaspoon salt
8 tablespoons (1 stick) unsalted butter, at room temperature
½ cup packed light brown sugar
¼ cup granulated sugar
1 large egg
1 cup prepared mincemeat
1 cup chopped walnuts

1. Preheat the oven to 325°F. Sift together the flour, baking soda, and salt in a bowl and set aside.

2. Cream together the butter, brown sugar, and granulated sugar in a large bowl. Whisk in the egg and make sure the mixture is smooth and well blended.

3. Mix the dry ingredients, a few tablespoons at a time, into the butter-sugar-egg mixture, making sure that each addition is fully incorporated before adding more. Stir in the mincemeat and walnuts, making sure the ingredients are evenly distributed.

4. Line a 9-inch round cake pan with parchment paper and butter the paper. (Don't worry too much about making it fit perfectly; the weight of the cake batter will do that job for you.) Pour in the cake batter, and bake until a knife inserted in the center comes out clean, about 1 hour. Serve warm. For an extra treat, top it with Custard Sauce (page 168).

PLUM PUDDING
Serves 8

Plum pudding is Britain's classic dried-fruit dessert. So why doesn't it have any plums in it? The recipe dates back to the time when plum meant any kind of dried fruit, and it has kept its name all through the centuries.

½ cup raisins
½ cup currants
½ cup chopped walnuts
¼ cup candied orange peel
¼ cup candied lemon peel
½ cup brandy or grappa
1 cup chopped tart apple, such as Granny Smith
¼ teaspoon ground cinnamon
¼ teaspoon ground mace
¼ teaspoon ground cloves
¼ teaspoon ground allspice
½ cup sugar
8 tablespoons (1 stick) unsalted butter, at room temperature
½ cup whole milk
2 large eggs, lightly beaten
½ cup unsulphured molasses
½ teaspoon baking soda
2 teaspoons baking powder
2 cups all-purpose flour
Custard Sauce (optional; page 168), for serving

1. Combine the raisins, currants, walnuts, orange peel, lemon peel, and brandy in a large bowl. Mix well and let the fruit and nuts soak until the liquid is well absorbed, about 4 hours.

2. Add the apple, cinnamon, mace, cloves, allspice, sugar, butter, milk, eggs, molasses, baking soda, baking powder, and flour, and mix well to form a smooth batter.

3. Oil a large heatproof bowl and pour in the batter. Pour about 1 inch of water into a pot with a cover that is large enough to hold the bowl. Put a metal trivet or large cookie cutter in the pot to support the bowl, and place the bowl on top. Cover, and bring to a simmer over medium-low heat. Steam the pudding until a toothpick inserted in the center comes out clean, about 2 hours. Check the water every 30 minutes or so to make sure there's enough there.

4. When the pudding is ready, remove it from the steaming pot, let it cool for 10 minutes, and unmold it onto a serving plate. Serve warm, with Custard Sauce, if you like.

St. Paul's Cathedral, London

POOR KNIGHTS *of* WINDSOR: EGGY BREAD

Makes 2 servings

Is French toast French? Perhaps, but it's actually a recipe that exists in lots of places. Poor Knights of Windsor, which also goes by the name eggy bread, is the British version, with a bit of sherry and without maple syrup. As for when to serve it, think of it as you would a crêpe, equally at home as a breakfast or dessert.

> 2 tablespoons superfine sugar
> 1 cup whole milk
> 3 tablespoons sherry
> 4 large eggs
> 8 slices day-old sandwich bread, crusts cut off
> 3 tablespoons unsalted butter
> 2 teaspoons ground cinnamon
> ¼ cup strawberry preserves (optional)

1. Combine 1 tablespoon of the sugar with the milk, sherry, and eggs in a shallow bowl and beat until smooth and well combined. Soak each slice of bread in the egg mixture, 1 or 2 at a time.

2. Melt 1 tablespoon of the butter in a skillet over medium heat. Pan-fry some slices of the soaked bread until it's nicely browned, about 4 minutes, and then turn them over and brown the other sides. Place the finished slices on individual plates. Using the remaining 2 tablespoons of butter as needed, continue until all 8 slices have been cooked.

3. Sprinkle the cooked toasts with the remaining tablespoon of sugar and the cinnamon. Spoon strawberry preserves on top, if you like, and serve right away.

SPOTTED DICK

Makes 4 servings

The fact that almost no one seems to know what it is does not
keep people from asking me regularly if I can make spotted
dick. It's a great dessert, rich and sweet, especially when served
with what the British call custard (Custard Sauce, page 168).

2 cups all-purpose flour
1 teaspoon baking powder
½ cup shredded beef suet or shortening
1 cup whole milk
½ cup packed brown sugar
1 cup raisins
1 tablespoon grated lemon zest
½ teaspoon salt
Custard Sauce (optional; page 168), for serving

1. Combine the flour, baking powder, and suet in a large
bowl and pinch them together with your fingers to form the
beginnings of a dough.

2. Add the milk, brown sugar, raisins, lemon zest, and
salt and mix with a wooden spoon until a thick, dough-like
batter forms.

3. Oil the insides of 4 heatproof 8-ounce cups (it's easiest
with oil spray), and spoon the dough into them. Pour about 1
inch of water into a pot with a cover that is large enough to
hold these cups. Put a metal trivet or large cookie cutter in the
pot to support the cups, and place the cups on top. Cover, bring
to a simmer over medium-low heat, and steam for 2 hours,
or until cooked all the way through. Check the water every
30 minutes or so to make sure there's enough there. Let the
puddings cool for 10 minutes.

4. Unmold the puddings onto dessert plates, and serve
warm, preferably with Custard Sauce.

TREACLE TART

Makes 1 (9-inch) tart, to serve 6

What do you think a treacle tart would be filled with? If it were a dish from any other cuisine, you might answer, "Treacle!" This is Britain though, so that can't be right. In fact, while treacle tarts may once have been filled with the stuff, today they're made with golden syrup, a similar, but far less complex product. It's available in British and Irish import shops; if you can't find it, use light Karo syrup instead.

2 cups cake flour, plus more if needed
2 tablespoons sugar
½ teaspoon salt
8 tablespoons (1 stick) unsalted butter, cut into small pieces
½ cup water, plus more if needed
2 cups golden syrup (preferable) or light Karo syrup
2 cups dried, unflavored bread crumbs
1 tablespoon grated lemon zest
2 tablespoons fresh lemon juice
1 tablespoon grated fresh ginger
¼ teaspoon ground cloves

1. Combine the flour with the sugar and ¼ teaspoon of the salt in a large bowl. Add the butter, and pinch with your fingers to blend with the flour mixture until you have something that looks like large bread crumbs.

2. Mix in the water and work the mixture with your hands until a smooth dough forms. If the dough is dry and cracking, add more water, 1 tablespoon at a time, until it becomes smooth. If the dough is too sticky, add flour, 1 tablespoon at a time, until you have a smooth dough.

3. Turn the dough out onto a floured work surface and knead it just long enough to eliminate lumps. Wrap the dough in plastic wrap and set it aside to rest for at least 30 minutes. Meanwhile, preheat the oven to 375°F.

4. Combine the golden syrup, the remaining ¼ teaspoon salt, the bread crumbs, lemon zest and juice, ginger, and cloves in a large bowl. Set aside.

5. Roll out the dough into a large disk about ½ inch thick. Place it in a 9-inch pie or tart pan. Use your fingers to press the dough into the curves of the pan, and then trim the edges. Give the syrup mixture one last stir, and then spoon into the pan. Bake the tart until the filling sets, about 40 minutes. Let cool for at least 10 minutes, and serve.

KENTISH HUFFKINS: YEAST-RAISED SWEET BREAD

Makes 8 rolls

Kentish huffkins are a great, slightly sweet bread to have with coffee or tea. Made with yeast and sugar, they are a Kentish spin on a scone.

  3 cups all-purpose flour
  1 teaspoon salt
  1 packet instant yeast (about 2¼ teaspoons)
  2 tablespoons unsalted butter, at room temperature
  1 cup whole milk
  2 teaspoons sugar

1. Combine the flour, salt, and yeast in a large bowl. Add the butter, and combine with the flour by pinching together bits of butter and flour with your fingers. You should wind up with something with the texture of bread crumbs. Add the milk and mix with a wooden spoon until a smooth dough forms.

2. Turn the dough out onto a floured work surface and knead it until it becomes elastic, about 6 minutes. Put the dough in an oiled bowl, cover with a tea towel, and leave in a warm, draft-free place until it doubles in size, about 2 hours.

3. Return the dough to a floured work surface. Punch down the dough, divide it into 8 equal portions, and roll each piece into a ball. Oil a baking sheet and place the balls of dough on it, at least 2 inches apart. Cover with a tea towel and put the sheet in a draft-free place until the dough doubles again in size, about 1 hour more. Meanwhile, preheat the oven to 450°F.

4. Use your thumb to make a dent in the top of each huffkin. Bake the rolls until their crusts are golden, about 15 minutes. Remove from the oven and let cool for 10 minutes before serving.

Church of St. John the Baptist, Cardiff, Wales

WELSH DRIPPING CAKE

Makes 1 (8-inch) round cake to serve 6

Is dripping cake Welsh? I'm not all that sure. Yes, it's a popular recipe in Wales, but it may well be that it gets the name from the frugality of using beef drippings in a cake. (To the English, the Welsh seem especially frugal.) Whether it's truly Welsh or not, it's a cake that shows that you can combine cheap staples like fat and flour with expensive goodies like dried fruit and wind up with a real treat.

½ cup beef drippings or lard
4 tablespoons (½ stick) unsalted butter, at room temperature
⅓ cup packed brown sugar
½ cup currants
½ cup raisins
½ cup candied lemon peel
½ cup candied orange peel
3 cups all-purpose flour, plus more if needed
1 teaspoon ground cinnamon
2 cups whole milk, plus more if needed
Hot tea (optional), for serving

1. Preheat the oven to 375°F. Cream together the drippings with the butter and brown sugar in a large bowl. Mix in the currants, raisins, lemon peel, and orange peel.

2. Add the flour, cinnamon, and milk and mix with a wooden spoon until you have something a bit thicker than a pancake batter. If it's too thin, add flour, 1 tablespoon at a time, to thicken it. If it's too thick, add milk, 1 tablespoon at a time, until it's right.

3. Pour the batter into a well-oiled 8-inch round cake pan. Bake the cake for 1 hour and 15 minutes, or until a knife inserted in the center comes out dry. Let cool for at least 15 minutes in the pan. Serve with hot tea if you like.

WHOLE-WHEAT SCONES

Makes 12 scones

Here's a whole-grain update of that longtime British favorite, the scone. Serve it with hot tea at any time of the day or evening.

4 cups whole-wheat flour, plus more if needed
2 tablespoons baking powder
1 teaspoon salt
8 tablespoons (1 stick) unsalted butter, cut into ½-inch pieces
1 cup packed light brown sugar
1 cup raisins
1½ cups buttermilk, plus more if needed
Jam (optional), for serving
Hot tea (optional), for serving

1. Preheat the oven to 325°F. Mix the flour, baking powder, and salt together in a large bowl. Add the butter and use your fingers to pinch the butter and the flour mixture together; when it's all combined, it will resemble large bread crumbs.

2. Use a wooden spoon to mix in the brown sugar and raisins, and then add the buttermilk. If the dough is quite sticky, add more flour, 1 tablespoon at a time, until the dough has the texture of modeling clay. If it's too dry, add more buttermilk, 1 tablespoon at a time, until it's wet enough.

3. Turn the dough out onto a floured work surface and roll it out into a rectangle ¼ inch thick. Cut the dough into 12 (3-inch) squares. Leftover scraps can be rerolled to make more scones.

4. Oil a baking sheet. Fold each square of dough in half diagonally to form a triangle, and lay it on the sheet. Bake the scones until the tops are golden brown, about 30 minutes. Serve warm, with jam and a pot of hot tea if you like.

The
PLOUGHMAN'S
CUPBOARD

I think it's surprising how infrequently people try to make their own condiments and other staples. It's easier than they think. Where I live on the East Coast of the United States, the "British" section of the supermarket offers a smattering of preserves and sauces. It seems that even otherwise frugal shoppers will buy expensive jars of these products without even considering the possibility of preparing them at home.

From chutney to lemon curd to clotted cream, the British always have something that they can put on something else to make it taste better. In a pub, chutney can go on a burger; at a bed-and-breakfast, lemon curd turns toast into something rich and elegant; and clotted cream on berries or scones is in a league of its own.

CLOTTED CREAM

Makes 1 cup

I think I once had it in my mind that clotted cream came from special cows that produced very rich milk, but was otherwise just like any other cream. It took a while before it dawned on me that clotting was a process—a way of removing water from the cream, it turned out—and that it was something that home cooks could do. Use raw cream if you can get it, or pasteurized if not. Make sure your cream is *not* ultrapasteurized, and that it has no additives. Most supermarket cream won't meet this standard; health-food stores or fancy-food stores are a better bet.

You'll also need a heatproof dish (I use a shallow Pyrex bowl), a medium-size saucepan you can use to rig a double boiler with a large surface area, a whisk, and a thermometer that reads in the 150° to 170°F range. Also, be aware that making clotted cream takes at least 3 hours.

3 cups heavy cream

1. Pour the cream into a heatproof dish or shallow bowl, and pour an inch or two of water into a saucepan that is large enough so that you can suspend the dish over it. Place the bowl over the saucepan, and then put the whole double boiler on the stove top over low heat.

2. Soon the cream will warm and skin over. Check the temperature, and make sure it remains between 150° and 170°F. Use a whisk to mix the skin back into the cream. Repeat this process every 10 minutes or so as each new skin forms, and keep an eye on the temperature; if the cream is too warm, it will scorch, and if it is too cool, the water in the cream will not evaporate and the cream will not thicken properly.

3. After about 3 hours, the cream will have reduced to about one-third of its original volume and be about the same consistency as melted ice cream. Remove it from the heat and pour it into ramekins or other individual dishes. Chill, covered, in the refrigerator for at least 30 minutes. Serve with fresh berries (strawberries are the classic here), or on baked goods (scones, such as the whole-wheat ones on page 186, are a favorite teatime choice). Or, even better, take a cue from the locals of Devon and put it on a baked potato. Stored in the refrigerator, clotted cream will keep for 1 week.

the clotter's diary

Americans by the thousands have traveled from one end of Devon to the other in search of clotted cream, the county's signature dairy topping. A few are smart enough to look in dairy farms, but most head to tea shops, where meals are offered and legends propagated. There your server will insist that cream somehow comes out of a cow, a very special Devonshire cow, in its clotted form. I just hope you don't believe them. So many people propagate the "special cow" theory of clotted cream that it's tough to ignore them. Is it a conspiracy? While there are lots of folks out there who want you to buy those tiny and insanely expensive jars sold in fancy shops, this book is on your side.

Since there's no such thing as a clottery, I couldn't just pay a visit to one and watch the process. I had to get myself some cream, research existing methods, and see how they tasted.

Getting unadulterated cream can be a tough task. The stuff sold in my local supermarket was so loaded with additives that concentrating it was out of the question. Luckily, some health- and fancy-food stores near me had unadulterated, yet still pasteurized, cream. Raw cream might have been better, but that would have required driving to another state.

I rejected recipes for clotted cream that faked the real thing by thickening cream with cream cheese or mascarpone. I concentrated on ones that appeared to be traditional, rooted in Devonshire regional cooking. There the method involves rigging a sort of double boiler that lets the cream sit in a relatively thin layer, to be warmed up over low heat until a skin forms. Then you stir the skin back into the liquid so that it thickens and yellows. You repeat until the cream is the consistency of melted ice cream and the color of parchment. When it cools, it clots.

On the first try, it didn't work out the way I'd hoped. Fearing a scorched mess, I kept the heat a bit too low and didn't let the cream reduce enough. I wound up with a great triple cream. I wanted clotted cream, though, not cheese.

For the second try, I skimmed off the skin on top of the cream and reserved it. This method—suggested by an otherwise reliable British-dairy website—resulted in a gelatinous mess. It didn't taste that bad; no extraction of pure cream could, unless it had been scorched. But it still wasn't clotted cream.

I gave it one more try. I enlisted the help of a thermometer and a whisk. This time I did not skim; the whisk would quickly break up and dissolve the skin. And some research indicated that the cream could be kept as warm as 170°F without scorching.

This method worked like a dream. While the clotted cream was still warm, I poured it over a baked potato. When it cooled off a bit, I spread it on a scone with jam. It was so filling that I couldn't eat anything else the rest of the day.

CUMBERLAND SAUCE

Makes 2 cups

Perfect over a slice of cold cooked ham, roast chicken, or salmon, Cumberland sauce uses sweetness and spice to make its point.

1 cup currant jelly
½ cup orange juice
2 tablespoons fresh lemon juice
¼ cup port
1 tablespoon grated orange zest
1 tablespoon grated lemon zest
1 tablespoon hot mustard powder
¼ teaspoon ground cloves
½ cup golden raisins

1. Combine the jelly, orange juice, lemon juice, and port in a saucepan over low heat and stir until the jelly liquefies and the other ingredients blend together.

2. Mix in the orange zest, lemon zest, mustard, cloves, and raisins. Stir until the ground cloves are dissolved in the sauce.

3. Gently simmer the mixture, uncovered, over low heat, stirring occasionally, until the raisins are plump, about 15 minutes. Transfer to a serving dish and chill, covered, in the refrigerator for at least 1 hour. Cumberland Sauce will keep in the refrigerator for at least 1 week. Warm it gently in a saucepan before serving.

GENTLEMAN'S RELISH

Makes ½ cup

What sort of relish would a true British gentleman eat? The answer, it turns out, is one that isn't anything like what any Americans I know would call relish in the first place. For one thing, it doesn't have vinegar, and for another, it has butter—lots of butter. And, finally, it has a lot more anchovies. One last thing: This recipe is top secret, so don't tell anybody where you found it.

¼ cup finely chopped oil-packed anchovy fillets
4 tablespoons (½ stick) unsalted butter, at room temperature
¼ teaspoon ground mace
¼ teaspoon hot chili powder
¼ teaspoon freshly ground black pepper

1. Combine the anchovies, butter, mace, chili powder, and black pepper in a bowl. Mash the ingredients together until they are evenly distributed; the back of a large wooden spoon works well for this.

2. Transfer the mixture to a jar or ramekin and let it chill in the refrigerator until the flavors combine, at least 2 hours. Serve at room temperature or chilled, on top of warm toast. Store, tightly covered, in the refrigerator, where it will keep for at least 2 weeks.

LEMON CURD

Makes 3 cups

A custard that takes the place of a jam, lemon curd is the richest and most unctuous thing you can put on a piece of toast. The British also use it often in place of jam as a filling for pastries, such as a roly-poly (page 165).

1 cup fresh lemon juice
3 tablespoons shredded lemon rind (both the zest and white pith)
5 large eggs, lightly beaten
8 tablespoons (1 stick) unsalted butter
3 cups sugar

1. Combine the lemon juice and rind, eggs, and butter in the top of a double boiler over low heat. Cook, stirring constantly, until a custard begins to form. (If you stop stirring, you'll have an omelet.)

2. Gradually stir in the sugar until it is completely dissolved. Then (and only then), stop stirring, and pour the finished curd into clean jars with lids. Store in the refrigerator, where it will keep for at least 2 weeks.

FRUIT CHUTNEY

Makes 3 cups

In homes, in sandwich shops, and in pubs across the British Isles, chutney is a universal condiment. Think of it as British salsa. Put it on a baguette, a slice of ham, or a big piece of cheese for a burst of flavor that's bolder than ketchup but tamer than hot sauce.

1 cup cider vinegar
½ cup finely chopped red onion
1 cup diced apple
1 cup diced pear
1 cup diced mango
½ cup chopped red bell pepper
½ cup golden raisins
2 tablespoons finely chopped fresh ginger
1 cup packed brown sugar
1 teaspoon curry powder
¼ teaspoon ground cinnamon
¼ teaspoon ground nutmeg
½ teaspoon salt

1. In a saucepan large enough to hold all the ingredients, bring the vinegar to a boil and stir in the onion, apple, pear, mango, bell pepper, raisins, ginger, and brown sugar. Reduce the heat to a simmer and cook, stirring frequently, for about 10 minutes, or until the fruit is soft and the sugar is completely dissolved.

2. Mix in the curry powder, cinnamon, nutmeg, and salt. Cook the chutney until all the flavors are well combined, about 30 minutes more. Serve warm or cold, or store, covered, in the refrigerator until ready to use. Chutney will keep for up to 2 weeks in the refrigerator.

PICKLED ONIONS

Makes 2 cups

Pickled onions are perfect alongside Fish and Chips (page 83), a ploughman's lunch (see sidebar, page 25), and all sorts of cold dishes. These onions are refrigerator pickles, meant to last a few weeks in the refrigerator in a lidded jar or other covered container. Add the chile pepper if you like the extra heat.

2 cups pearl onions
1 cup cider vinegar
1 teaspoon salt
1 teaspoon whole black peppercorns
½ teaspoon whole allspice
2 whole cloves
½ teaspoon mustard seeds
1 dried whole chile pepper (optional)
Water, as needed

1. To peel the pearl onions, put them in boiling water for 30 seconds, drain them immediately, and transfer them to a bowl of cold water. Once they are cool enough to handle, drain them again and remove their skins by hand.

2. Combine the vinegar, salt, peppercorns, allspice, cloves, mustard seeds, and chile pepper, if using, in a saucepan. Bring the vinegar to a boil over high heat, and continue boiling for 1 minute. Remove from the heat and set aside.

3. Put the onions in a wide-mouth lidded glass or plastic container, and add the vinegar-spice mixture. If there is not enough liquid to cover the onions, add water, 1 tablespoon at a time, until you have the right amount.

4. Cover tightly and store in the refrigerator. The onions will be ready to eat after 3 days and will keep for at least 2 weeks.

A MODEST GLOSSARY
of BRITISH FOOD TERMS

═══════════════

Here is a short glossary of British food words that are likely to be unfamiliar to Americans. Some are used in the text of this book, while others are ones that you might encounter when you cook, dine, or shop in Great Britain. If this book also kindles your interest in exploring British food and recipes in other print or online sources, I hope you will find this to be a useful reference.

british word	u.s. meaning
Aubergine	Eggplant
Banger	A large, mildly seasoned fresh sausage. Make sure you get yours from a good butcher. Serve with mashed potatoes for bangers and mash.
Bap	A cross between a hamburger bun and a sandwich roll
Beetroot	Beet
Biscuit	Cookie
Broad bean	Fava bean
Brown bread	Whole-wheat bread
Bully beef	Canned corned beef
Butty	Sandwich on a roll
Candy floss	Cotton candy
Caster sugar	Confectioners' sugar
Chipolata	A small, mild sausage
Chocolate vermicelli	Chocolate sprinkles
Cider	Fruit-based beverage that is always hard (alcoholic), never just a juice
Cornflour	Cornstarch
Courgette	Zucchini
Crisps	Potato chips
Crumpet	In England, something similar to an American "English muffin." In Scotland, a type of pancake.
Demerara sugar	Coarse, raw sugar. Substitute either turbinado or light brown sugar.
Double cream	Heavy cream
Faggot	Meatball
Fairy cake	Cupcake

british word	u.s. meaning
Fish finger	Fish stick
Gammon or gammon steak	Ham steak
Golden syrup	A light sugar syrup; substitute light Karo syrup for it.
Grilled	Broiled
Jacket potato	Baked potato
Marrow	A large squash
Mince	Ground meat, usually beef
Perry	Pear cider
Prawn	Shrimp
Punnet	A basket-like container in which berries and other small produce items are sold at farmers' markets
Salad cream	Salad dressing—especially prepared commercial salad dressing, usually similar to American ranch dressing
Salt beef	Corned beef
Sauce	Condiment
Single cream	Light cream
Sponge finger	Ladyfinger
Squash	Fruit-flavored drink or punch
Sultana	Golden raisin
Swede	Turnip
Treacle	A dark sugar syrup, somewhat similar to molasses
White stock	Chicken stock

Acknowledgments

Recreating a foreign cuisine in an American kitchen is always a challenge. Luckily, it was one that I did not have to face alone. Two old friends, Bob Croxford in Cornwall and Simon Evans in Shrewsbury, answered many of my questions and offered local perspective. In London, my in-laws Giovanna Asselle and Suhas Shanbhag and dear friends Ling and Emory Anderson always opened their doors and kitchens for me.

Not only did friends and relatives pitch in, experts did, too. Elaine, the pasty guru from Padstow, Cornwall, the entire staff (and most of the customers) at Popular Balti in Birmingham, Doug from the Carron Fish Bar in Stonehaven, and Eric from the Trumland Organic Farm on Rousay, Orkney, all gave freely of their time and knowledge.

Here in the States, our small band of British food lovers pitched in, too. Chris Sell from the Chipshop in Brooklyn, New York; Richard Penfold, the fish smoker, from Stonington, Maine; Barbara and Dave at the British Connection, a terrific New Jersey specialty store; and tea expert Judith Krall-Russo (who turned out to be a neighbor of mine), all took the time to share their enthusiasm and skills.

Getting this book into print was no easy task. Michael Bourret, my agent, made sure that things moved forward, even when the weight of the world was pushing us the other way. At the Harvard Common Press, Valerie Cimino, Dan Rosenberg, Pat Jalbert-Levine, and Virginia Downes worked hard to bring the project to life. I thank all of you for turning my notes and scratches into a real book.

Measurement Equivalents

LIQUID CONVERSIONS

U.S.	Metric
1 tsp	5 ml
1 tbs	15 ml
2 tbs	30 ml
3 tbs	45 ml
1/4 cup	60 ml
1/3 cup	75 ml
1/3 cup + 1 tbs	90 ml
1/3 cup + 2 tbs	100 ml
1/2 cup	120 ml
2/3 cup	150 ml
3/4 cup	180 ml
3/4 cup + 2 tbs	200 ml
1 cup	240 ml
1 cup + 2 tbs	275 ml
1 1/4 cups	300 ml
1 1/3 cups	325 ml
1 1/2 cups	350 ml
1 2/3 cups	375 ml
1 3/4 cups	400 ml
1 3/4 cups + 2 tbs	450 ml
2 cups (1 pint)	475 ml
2 1/2 cups	600 ml
3 cups	720 ml
4 cups (1 quart)	945 ml
(1,000 ml is 1 liter)	

WEIGHT CONVERSIONS

U.S./U.K.	Metric
1/2 oz	14 g
1 oz	28 g
1 1/2 oz	43 g
2 oz	57 g
2 1/2 oz	71 g
3 oz	85 g
3 1/2 oz	100 g
4 oz	113 g
5 oz	142 g
6 oz	170 g
7 oz	200 g
8 oz	227 g
9 oz	255 g
10 oz	284 g
11 oz	312 g
12 oz	340 g
13 oz	368 g
14 oz	400 g
15 oz	425 g
1 lb	454 g

OVEN TEMPERATURE CONVERSIONS

°F	Gas Mark	°C
250	1/2	120
275	1	140
300	2	150
325	3	165
350	4	180
375	5	190
400	6	200
425	7	220
450	8	230
475	9	240
500	10	260
550	Broil	290

NOTE: All conversions are approximate.

Index

Note: Page references in *italics* indicate recipe photographs.

A

Almond and Prune Stuffing, Chicken with (Lancashire
     Hindle Wakes), 78–79, *79*
Anchovies
     in English cooking, 31
     Fish Cakes, 86, *87*
     Gentleman's Relish, 193
     Salmagundi, 30, *30*
     Scotch Woodcock, 12, *12*
Apples
     Cumberland Pudding, 166, *167*
     Fidget Pie, 151, *151*
     Fruit Chutney, 195, *195*
     Plum Pudding, 178
Apricot(s)
     Coronation Chicken, 18, *18*
     and Walnut Stuffing, Roast Pork with, 90
Asparagus, Potted, 31

B

Bacon
     American definition of, 91
     British definition of, 91
     Faggots, 93, *93*
     Fidget Pie, 151, *151*
     Galantine of Chicken, 20, *20*
     Pease Porridge, 129
     Roly-Poly, 138, *138*

Balti
     One-Pot, 106, *107*
     origins of, 104–105
Bananas
     Banoffee Pie, 169
Banoffee Pie, 169
Barley and Lamb Soup, Scotch (Scotch Broth), 43
Beans, Baked, British-Style, 7
Bed-and-breakfast inns, about, 8, 173
Beef
     Boiled, 64
     Bubble and Squeak: Fried Cabbage, Potatoes, and Corned
          Beef, 128, *128*
     Cockney-Style Minced Meat Pie, 142
     Collops with Pickled Walnuts, 65, *65*
     Cottage Pie, 145
     Dumplings and Mince, 67
     Faggots, 93, *93*
     Rag Pudding, 96, *97*
     Roast, Classic, with Gravy, 68, *69*
     Steak and Kidney Pie, *148*, 149
     Tea, 42, *42*
     Traditional Cornish Steak Pasty, 156, *157*
     Tripe and Onions, *98*, 99
     Wellington, *62*, 63, *63*
Bhaji, Onion, 114, *114*
Biryani, Shrimp, 116, *116*
Biscuits. *See* Cookies and bars
Black Pudding, 10
Boiled Beef, 64

Borough Market (London), 122–123
Bread
    Eggy (Poor Knights of Windsor), 180, *180*
    Fried, 6, *6*
    Hot Cross Buns, 175
    Sweet, Yeast-Raised (Kentish Huffkins), 183
    Whole-Wheat Scones, 186, *187*
    Yorkshire Pudding, *158–159*, 159
Breakfast
    Black Pudding, 10
    British-Style Baked Beans, 7
    Fried Bread, 6, *6*
    full English, about, 4–5, 13
    Grilled Tomatoes, 13
    Jugged Kippers, 11, *11*
    Kedgeree, 9, *9*
    Poor Knights of Windsor: Eggy Bread, 180, *180*
    Scotch Woodcock, 12, *12*
Brooklyn, New York, fish-and-chips, 38–39
Bubble and Squeak: Fried Cabbage, Potatoes, and Corned
    Beef, 128, *128*
Buns and rolls
    Hot Cross Buns, 175
    Kentish Huffkins: Yeast-Raised Sweet Bread, 183

C

Cabbage
    Bubble and Squeak: Fried Cabbage, Potatoes, and Corned
        Beef, 128, *128*
    Colcannon (variation), 128
    Scotch Oatmeal Soup, 47, *47*
    Vegetarian Shepherd's Pie, 146, *147*
Cake(s)
    Mincemeat, 177, *177*
    Welsh Dripping, 185, *185*
Carrots
    Garden Vegetable Pasty, 160

Vegetarian Shepherd's Pie, 146, *147*
Cashews
    Shrimp Biryani, 116, *116*
Cauliflower
    One-Pot Balti, 106, *107*
Cawl, origins of, 73–75
Cawl: Welsh Lamb Stew, 71, *71*
Cawl Cennin: Welsh-Style Leek and Potato Soup, 55, *55*
Cheddar cheese
    Leek Pie, 143
    Pan Haggerty, 126
    Staffordshire Oatcakes, 35, *35*
    Welsh Rarebit, *132*, 133
Cheese. *See* Cheddar cheese
Chicken
    Coronation, 18, *18*
    Galantine of, 20, *20*
    Ham, and Mushroom Pie, 139, *139*
    Hash, Scottish (Dunelm), 81
    Korma, 103
    Leek, and Prune Soup (Cock-a-Leekie), 44, *45*
    and Leek Casserole, 76, *77*
    Mulligatawny Soup, 50
    with Prune and Almond Stuffing (Lancashire Hindle
        Wakes), 78–79, *79*
    Roast, Scottish (Howtowdie), 80, *80*
    Salmagundi, 30, *30*
    Tikka Masala, 110
Chickpea flour
    Onion Bhaji, 114, *114*
Chipshop, 38–39
Chutney, Fruit, 195, *195*
Clapshot, *124*, 125
Clotted Cream, *190*, 191
Clotted cream, about, 192
Cock-a-Leekie: Chicken, Leek, and Prune Soup, 44, *45*
Cockney-Style Minced Meat Pie, 142

Coconut
    Chicken Korma, 103
    Flapjacks, 172, *172*
    Shrimp Biryani, 116, *116*
Colcannon (variation), 128
Cookies and bars
    Fat Rascals, *170,* 171
    Flapjacks, 172, *172*
    Spicy Gingersnaps, 174, *174*
Cornish Steak Pasty, Traditional, 156, *157*
Coronation Chicken, 18, *18*
Cottage Pie, 145
Crab
    Deviled, 37, *37*
    Soup, Scottish, Cream of (Partan Bree), 56
Cream, Clotted, *190,* 191
Cream, clotted, about, 192
Crust, British Hot-Water, 137
Cucumber and Salmon Sandwich, 36, *36*
Cullen Skink: Smoked Haddock and Potato
    Soup, 57
Cumberland Pudding, 166, *167*
Cumberland Sauce, 193
Cupboard items
    Clotted Cream, *190,* 191
    Cumberland Sauce, 193
    Fruit Chutney, 195, *195*
    Gentleman's Relish, 193
    Lemon Curd, 194, *194*
    Pickled Onions, 197, *197*
Curd, Lemon, 194, *194*
Currants
    Cumberland Pudding, 166, *167*
    Fat Rascals, *170,* 171
    Hot Cross Buns, 175
    Plum Pudding, 178
    Welsh Dripping Cake, 185, *185*

Curry dishes
    Balti, origins of, 104–105
    British curry, origins of, 102
    Chicken Korma, 103
    Chicken Tikka Masala, 110
    Coronation Chicken, 18, *18*
    Kedgeree, 9, *9*
    Lamb Dopiaza, 109
    Mulligatawny Soup, 50
    One-Pot Balti, 106, *107*
    phal, about, 117
    Scottish Rabbit Curry, *118,* 119
    Shrimp Biryani, 116, *116*
    Tofu Tikka Masala, 113, *113*
Custard Sauce, 168, *168*

D

Desserts. *See* Sweets
Deviled Crab, 37, *37*
Dips and spreads
    Gentleman's Relish, 193
    Kipper Pâté, 24, *24*
    Lemon Curd, 194, *194*
    Onion Relish, 114
    Potted Asparagus, 31
    Potted Ham, 27
Dopiaza, Lamb, 109
Dripping Cake, Welsh, 185, *185*
Dumplings and Mince, 67
Dunelm: Scottish Chicken Hash, 81

E

Eels, cooking, 140–141
Eggs
    Kedgeree, 9, *9*
    Pickled, *26,* 27
    Salmagundi, 30, *30*

Scotch, 28, *29*
Scotch Woodcock, 12, *12*

F

Faggots, 93, *93*
Fat Rascals, *170*, 171
Ffest y Cybydd: Miser's Feast, 92
Fidget Pie, 151, *151*
Fish. *See also* Anchovies; Shellfish
    Cakes, 86, *87*
    and Chips, *82*, 83
    Cream, Jellied, 19, *19*
    Cullen Skink: Smoked Haddock and Potato Soup, 57
    fish-and-chip shops, 84–85
    Fried Smelts, 89, *89*
    Jugged Kippers, 11, *11*
    Kedgeree, 9, *9*
    Kipper Pâté, 24, *24*
    Pie with Mashed Potato Crust, 153, *153*
    Salmon and Cucumber Sandwich, 36, *36*
    Salmon Broth, *48*, 49
    smoked, in Stonington, Maine, 22–23
Flapjacks, 172, *172*
Fruit. *See also specific fruits*
    Chutney, 195, *195*
    Trifle, 173
    Welsh Dripping Cake, 185, *185*

G

Galantine of Chicken, 20, *20*
Garlic
    Masala Sauce, 111, *111*
    Tofu Tikka Masala, 113, *113*
Gentleman's Relish, 193
Ginger
    Masala Sauce, 111, *111*
    Spicy Gingersnaps, 174, *174*

Tofu Tikka Masala, 113, *113*
Grains. *See* Barley; Oats; Rice
Gravy, Parsley (Liquor), 143
Greens
    Cream of Watercress Soup, 46
    Scotch Broth: Lamb and Barley Soup, 43

H

Haddock
    Kedgeree, 9, *9*
    Smoked, and Potato Soup (Cullen Skink), 57
Haggis, about, 60–61
Ham
    Chicken, and Mushroom Pie, 139, *139*
    Potted, 27
    Salmagundi, 30, *30*
Herring, smoked. *See* Kipper(s)
Hot Cross Buns, 175
Howtowdie: Scottish Roast Chicken, 80, *80*
Huffkins, Kentish: Yeast-Raised Sweet Bread, 183

I

Irish Hotpot (variation), 70

J

Jellied Fish Cream, 19, *19*

K

Kedgeree, 9, *9*
Kentish Huffkins: Yeast-Raised Sweet Bread, 183
Kidneys, lamb
    Rag Pudding, 96, *97*
    Steak and Kidney Pie, *148*, 149
Kipper(s)
    Jugged, 11, *11*
    Kedgeree, 9, *9*
    Pâté, 24, *24*

L

Lamb
and Barley Soup (Scotch Broth), 43
Cawl: Welsh Lamb Stew, 71, *71*
Dopiaza, 109
Lamb's Tongue with Raisin Sauce, *94*, 95
Lancashire Hotpot, 70, *70*
or Mutton Pie, 150
Rag Pudding, 96, *97*
Shepherd's Pie, 145
Steak and Kidney Pie, *148*, 149
Lancashire Hindle Wakes: Chicken with Prune and Almond
Stuffing, 78–79, *79*
Lancashire Hotpot, 70, *70*
Leek
Chicken, and Prune Soup (Cock-a-Leekie), 44, *45*
and Chicken Casserole, 76, *77*
Pie, 143
and Potato Soup, Welsh-Style (Cawl Cennin), 55, *55*
Legumes
British-Style Baked Beans, 7
marrowfat peas, about, 130
Mushy Peas, 130, *131*
Pease Porridge, 129
Scotch Broth: Lamb and Barley Soup, 43
Lemon Curd, 194, *194*
Liquor: Parsley Gravy, 143
Liver
Faggots, 93, *93*

M

Main dishes
Beef Collops with Pickled Walnuts, 65, *65*
Beef Wellington, 62, 63, *63*
Boiled Beef, 64
Bubble and Squeak: Fried Cabbage, Potatoes, and Corned
Beef, 128, *128*

Cawl: Welsh Lamb Stew, 71, *71*
Chicken, Ham, and Mushroom Pie, 139, *139*
Chicken and Leek Casserole, 76, *77*
Chicken Korma, 103
Chicken Tikka Masala, 110
Classic Roast Beef with Gravy, 68, *69*
Cockney-Style Minced Meat Pie, 142
Cottage Pie, 145
Deviled Crab, 37, *37*
Dumplings and Mince, 67
Dunelm: Scottish Chicken Hash, 81
Faggots, 93, *93*
Ffest y Cybydd: Miser's Feast, 92
Fidget Pie, 151, *151*
Fish and Chips, 82, 83
Fish Cakes, 86, *87*
Fish Pie with Mashed Potato Crust, 153, *153*
Fried Smelts, 89, *89*
Garden Vegetable Pasty, 160
Howtowdie: Scottish Roast Chicken, 80, *80*
Irish Hotpot (variation), 70
Kedgeree, 9, *9*
Lamb Dopiaza, 109
Lamb's Tongue with Raisin Sauce, *94*, 95
Lancashire Hindle Wakes: Chicken with Prune and
Almond Stuffing, 78–79, *79*
Lancashire Hotpot, 70, *70*
Mutton or Lamb Pie, 150
One-Pot Balti, 106, *107*
Pan Haggerty, 126
Rag Pudding, 96, *97*
Roast Pork with Apricot and Walnut Stuffing, 90
Salmagundi, 30, *30*
Scottish Rabbit Curry, *118*, 119
Shepherd's Pie, 145
Shrimp Biryani, 116, *116*
Steak and Kidney Pie, 148, 149

Toad-in-the-Hole, 161, *161*

Tofu Tikka Masala, 113, *113*

Traditional Cornish Steak Pasty, 156, *157*

Tripe and Onions, 98, 99

Vegetarian Shepherd's Pie, 146, *147*

Marrowfat peas

  about, 130

  Mushy Peas, 130, *131*

Masala Sauce, 111, *111*

Meat. *See also* Beef; Lamb; Organ meats; Pork

  Scottish Rabbit Curry, *118*, 119

Minced Meat Pie, Cockney-Style, 142

Mincemeat Cake, 177, *177*

Miser's Feast (Ffest y Cybydd), 92

Mulligatawny Soup, 50

Mushroom(s)

  Beef Collops with Pickled Walnuts, 65, *65*

  Beef Wellington, *62*, 63, *63*

  Chicken, and Ham Pie, 139, *139*

  Dunelm: Scottish Chicken Hash, 81

  Garden Vegetable Pasty, 160

  Scottish Rabbit Curry, *118*, 119

  Staffordshire Oatcakes, 35, *35*

  Steak and Kidney Pie, *148*, 149

  Vegetarian Shepherd's Pie, 146, *147*

Mushy Peas, 130, *131*

Mutton or Lamb Pie, 150

N

Nuts

  Beef Collops with Pickled Walnuts, 65, *65*

  Flapjacks, 172, *172*

  Lancashire Hindle Wakes: Chicken with Prune and
    Almond Stuffing, 78–79, *79*

  Mincemeat Cake, 177, *177*

  Plum Pudding, 178

  Roast Pork with Apricot and Walnut Stuffing, 90

Shrimp Biryani, 116, *116*

O

Oatcakes, Staffordshire

  buying, 32–33

  recipe for, 35, *35*

Oats

  Flapjacks, 172, *172*

  Howtowdie: Scottish Roast Chicken, 80, *80*

  Scotch Oatmeal Soup, 47, *47*

Onion(s)

  Beef Collops with Pickled Walnuts, 65, *65*

  Bhaji, 114, *114*

  in British cooking, 115

  Ffest y Cybydd: Miser's Feast, 92

  Fidget Pie, 151, *151*

  Lamb Dopiaza, 109

  Masala Sauce, 111, *111*

  Pan Haggerty, 126

  Pickled, 197, *197*

  Relish, 115

  Scottish Rabbit Curry, *118*, 119

  slow cooking, 114

  Traditional Cornish Steak Pasty, 156, *157*

  Tripe and, 98, 99

  Vegetarian Shepherd's Pie, 146, *147*

Organ meats

  Faggots, 93, *93*

  Rag Pudding, 96, *97*

  Steak and Kidney Pie, *148*, 149

  Tripe and Onions, 98, 99

P

Pan Haggerty, 126

Parsley Gravy (Liquor), 143

Partan Bree: Scottish Cream of Crab
  Soup, 56

Pasty(ies)
    about, 154–155
    Cornish Steak, Traditional, 156, *157*
    Garden Vegetable, 160
    variations, ideas for, 160
Pâté, Kipper, 24, *24*
Peas
    Cottage Pie, 145
    Garden Vegetable Pasty, 160
    Jellied Fish Cream, 19, *19*
    Marrowfat, about, 130
    Mushy, 130, *131*
    Shepherd's Pie, 145
    Shrimp Biryani, 116, *116*
Peas, Split
    Pease Porridge, 129
    Scotch Broth: Lamb and Barley Soup, 43
Pease Porridge, 129
Penfold, Richard, 22–23
Peppers
    Fruit Chutney, 195, *195*
    One-Pot Balti, 106, *107*
Phal, about, 117
Pickled Eggs, 26, *27*
Pickled Onions, 197, *197*
Pickled Walnuts, Beef Collops with, 65, *65*
Pie and mash shops, in London, 140–141
Pie crusts
    British Hot-Water Crust, 137
Pies (savory)
    Bacon Roly-Poly, 138, *138*
    Chicken, Ham, and Mushroom, 139, *139*
    Cottage, 145
    Fidget, 151, *151*
    Fish, with Mashed Potato Crust, 153, *153*
    Garden Vegetable Pasty, 160
    Leek, 143

Minced Meat, Cockney-Style, 142
Mutton or Lamb, 150
pasties, about, 154–155
pasty variations, ideas for, 160
Shepherd's, 145
Steak and Kidney, *148*, 149
Traditional Cornish Steak Pasty, 156, *157*
Vegetarian Shepherd's Pie, 146, *147*
Pies (sweet)
    Banoffee, 169
Ploughman's lunch, assembling, 25, *25*
Plum Pudding, 178
Poor Knights of Windsor: Eggy Bread, 180, *180*
Pork. *See also* Bacon; Ham; Sausage(s)
    English bacon, about, 91
    Faggots, 93, *93*
    Ffest y Cybydd: Miser's Feast, 92
    Irish Hotpot (variation), 70
    Roast, with Apricot and Walnut Stuffing, 90
Port wine
    Cumberland Sauce, 193
Potato(es)
    Bubble and Squeak: Fried Cabbage, Potatoes, and Corned Beef, 128, *128*
    Clapshot, *124*, 125
    Colcannon (variation), 128
    Cottage Pie, 145
    Ffest y Cybydd: Miser's Feast, 92
    Fish and Chips, 82, *83*
    Fish Cakes, 86, *87*
    Garden Vegetable Pasty, 160
    Irish Hotpot (variation), 70
    Lancashire Hotpot, 70, *70*
    and Leek Soup, Welsh-Style (Cawl Cennin), 55, *55*
    Mashed, Crust, Fish Pie with, 153, *153*
    Pan Haggerty, 126
    Shepherd's Pie, 145

and Smoked Haddock Soup (Cullen Skink), 57
Traditional Cornish Steak Pasty, 156, *157*
Vegetarian Shepherd's Pie, 146, *147*
Potted Asparagus, 31
Potted Ham, 27
Poultry. *See* Chicken
Prune
    and Almond Stuffing, Chicken with (Lancashire Hindle
        Wakes), 78–79, *79*
    Chicken, and Leek Soup (Cock-a-Leekie), 44, *45*
Pubs (public houses), about, 125
Pudding
    Cumberland, 166, *167*
    Plum, 178
    Rag, 96, *97*
    Spotted Dick, 181, *181*
    Yorkshire, *158–159*, 159

R

Rabbit Curry, Scottish, *118*, 119
Rag Pudding, 96, *97*
Raisin(s)
    Cumberland Sauce, 193
    Flapjacks, 172, *172*
    Fruit Chutney, 195, *195*
    Plum Pudding, 178
    Roast Pork with Apricot and Walnut Stuffing, 90
    Sauce, Lamb's Tongue with, *94*, 95
    Shrimp Biryani, 116, *116*
    Spotted Dick, 181, *181*
    Welsh Dripping Cake, 185, *185*
    Whole-Wheat Scones, 186, *187*
Relish
    Gentleman's, 193
    Onion, 115
Rice
    Kedgeree, 9, *9*

Partan Bree: Scottish Cream of Crab Soup, 56
Shrimp Biryani, 116, *116*
Roly-Poly, Bacon, 138, *138*
Roly-Poly, Baked Jam, 165

S

Salads
    Coronation Chicken, 18, *18*
    Jellied Fish Cream, 19, *19*
    Salmagundi, 30, *30*
Salmagundi, 30, *30*
Salmon
    Broth, *48*, 49
    and Cucumber Sandwich, 36, *36*
    Fish Pie with Mashed Potato Crust, 153, *153*
    Jellied Fish Cream, 19, *19*
Sandwich(es)
    Coronation Chicken, 18, *18*
    Salmon and Cucumber, 36, *36*
    Welsh Rarebit, *132*, 133
Sauce(s)
    Cumberland, 193
    Custard, 168, *168*
    Masala, 111, *111*
Sausage(s)
    Black Pudding, 10
    Galantine of Chicken, 20, *20*
    haggis, about, 60–61
    Scotch Eggs, 28, *29*
    Staffordshire Oatcakes, 35, *35*
    Toad-in-the-Hole, 161, *161*
Scones, Whole-Wheat, 186, *187*
Scotch Broth: Lamb and Barley Soup, 43
Scotch Eggs, 28, *29*
Scotch Oatmeal Soup, 47, *47*
Scotch Woodcock, 12, *12*
Scottish Chicken Hash (Dunelm), 81

Scottish Cream of Crab Soup (Partan Bree), 56
Scottish Rabbit Curry, *118*, 119
Scottish Roast Chicken (Howtowdie), 80, *80*
Seafood. *See* Fish; Shellfish
Shellfish
    Deviled Crab, 37, *37*
    Fish Pie with Mashed Potato Crust, 153, *153*
    Partan Bree: Scottish Cream of Crab Soup, 56
    Shrimp Biryani, 116, *116*
Shepherd's Pie, 145
Shepherd's Pie, Vegetarian, 146, *147*
Shrimp
    Biryani, 116, *116*
    Fish Pie with Mashed Potato Crust, 153, *153*
Side dishes
    Clapshot, *124*, 125
    Colcannon (variation), 128
    Mushy Peas, 130, *131*
    Pan Haggerty, 126
    Pease Porridge, 129
    Welsh Rarebit, *132*, 133
    Yorkshire Pudding, *158–159*, 159
Smelts, Fried, 89, *89*
Smoked Haddock and Potato Soup (Cullen Skink), 57
Soup(s)
    Beef Tea, 42, *42*
    Cawl Cennin: Welsh-Style Leek and Potato Soup,
        55, *55*
    Cock-a-Leekie: Chicken, Leek, and Prune Soup, 44, *45*
    Cullen Skink: Smoked Haddock and Potato Soup, 57
    Mulligatawny, 50
    Partan Bree: Scottish Cream of Crab Soup, 56
    Salmon Broth, *48*, 49
    Scotch Broth: Lamb and Barley Soup, 43
    Scotch Oatmeal, 47, *47*
    Watercress, Cream of, 46
Spicy Gingersnaps, 174, *174*

Split Peas
    Pease Porridge, 129
    Scotch Broth: Lamb and Barley Soup, 43
Spotted Dick, 181, *181*
Staffordshire Oatcakes, 32–33
    recipe for, 35, *35*
Stews
    Cawl: Welsh Lamb Stew, 71, *71*
    Scottish Rabbit Curry, *118*, 119
Stonington, Maine, smoked fish, 22–23
Strawberry jam
    Baked Jam Roly-Poly, 165
    Fruit Trifle, 173
Sweets
    Baked Jam Roly-Poly, 165
    Banoffee Pie, 169
    Cumberland Pudding, 166, *167*
    Custard Sauce, 168, *168*
    deep-fried candy bars, about, 164
    Fat Rascals, *170*, 171
    Flapjacks, 172, *172*
    Fruit Trifle, 173
    Hot Cross Buns, 175
    Kentish Huffkins: Yeast-Raised Sweet Bread, 183
    Mincemeat Cake, 177, *177*
    Plum Pudding, 178
    Poor Knights of Windsor: Eggy Bread, 180, *180*
    Spicy Gingersnaps, 174, *174*
    Spotted Dick, 181, *181*
    Treacle Tart, 182, *182*
    Welsh Dripping Cake, 185, *185*
    Whole-Wheat Scones, 186, *187*

T

Tart, Treacle, 182, *182*
Tea
    Beef, 42, *42*

high tea, about, 16–17, 136
low tea, about, 16
    serving, 16–17
Toad-in-the-Hole, 161, *161*
Tofu Tikka Masala, 113, *113*
Tomatoes
    Grilled, 13
    Masala Sauce, 111, *111*
Tongue, Lamb's, with Raisin Sauce, 94, 95
Travel. *See* United Kingdom food and travel
Treacle Tart, 182, *182*
Trifle, Fruit, 173
Tripe and Onions, 98, 99
Turnips
    Clapshot, *124*, 125
    Garden Vegetable Pasty, 160
    Traditional Cornish Steak Pasty, 156, *157*

U

United Kingdom food and travel
    anchovies, in English cooking, 31
    Balti, origins of, 104–105
    bed-and-breakfast inns, about, 8, 173
    Borough Market (London), 122–123
    British curry, origins of, 102
    British definition of bacon, 91
    buying Staffordshire Oatcakes, 32–33
    cawl, origins of, 73–75
    clotted cream, about, 192
    deep-fried candy bars, about, 164
    fish-and-chip shops, 84–85
    fried foods, 38–39
    full English breakfasts, 4–5, 13
    Haggis, about, 60–61
    high tea, about, 16–17, 136
    London pie and mash shops, 140–141

low tea, about, 16
onions, in British cooking, 114
pasties, about, 154–155
phal, about, 117
Ploughman's lunch, assembling, 25, *25*
pubs (public houses), about, 125
Rousay Island, about, 52–53
serving tea, 16–17
tea trays in, 173
West Country, about, 152

V

Vegetable(s). *See also specific vegetables*
    Garden, Pasty, 160
    Vegetarian Shepherd's Pie, 146, *147*

W

Walnut(s)
    and Apricot Stuffing, Roast Pork with, 90
    Mincemeat Cake, 177, *177*
    Pickled, Beef Collops with, 65, *65*
    Plum Pudding, 178
Watercress Soup, Cream of, 46
Welsh Dripping Cake, 185, *185*
Welsh Lamb Stew (Cawl), 71, *71*
Welsh Rarebit, *132*, 133
Welsh-Style Leek and Potato Soup (Cawl Cennin),
    55, *55*
Whole-Wheat Scones, 186, *187*

Y

Yogurt
    Chicken Korma, 103
    Chicken Tikka Masala, 110
    Tofu Tikka Masala, 113, *113*
Yorkshire Pudding, *158–159*, 159